THE CRITICS DEBATE

General Editor: Michael Scott

The Critics Debate

General Editor Michael Scott

Published titles:

HENRY IV
Parts I & II

Ronald Knowles

M
MACMILLAN

First published 1992 by
THE MACMILLAN PRESS LTD
Houndmills, Basingstoke, Hampshire RG21 2XS
and London
Companies and representatives
throughout the world

ISBN 0–333–52579–5 hardcover
ISBN 0–333–52580–9 paperback

A catalogue record for this book is available
from the British Library.

Typeset by Footnote Graphics,
Warminster, Wiltshire

Printed in Hong Kong

Contents

General Editor's Preface

OVER THE last few years the practice of literary criticism has become hotly debated. Methods developed earlier in the century and before have been attacked and the word 'crisis' has been drawn upon to describe the present condition of English Studies. That such a debate is taking place is a sign of the subject discipline's health. Some would hold that the situation necessitates a radical alternative approach which naturally implies a 'crisis situation'. Others would respond that to employ such terms is to precipitate or construct a false position. The debate continues but it is not the first. 'New Criticism' acquired its title because it attempted something fresh, calling into question certain practices of the past. Yet the practices it attacked were not entirely lost or negated by the new critics. One factor becomes clear: English Studies is a pluralistic discipline.

What are students coming to advanced work in English for the first time to make of all this debate and controversy? They are in danger of being overwhelmed by the cross-currents of critical approaches as they take up their study of literature. The purpose of this series is to help delineate various critical approaches to specific literary texts. Its authors are from a variety of critical schools and have approached their task in a flexible manner. Their aim is to help the reader come to terms with the variety of criticism and to introduce him or her to further reading on the subject and to a fuller evaluation of a particular text by illustrating the way it has been approached in a number of contexts. In the first part of the book a critical survey is given of some of the major ways the text has been appraised. This is done sometimes in a thematic manner, sometimes according to various 'schools' or 'approaches'. In the second part the authors provide their own appraisals of the text from their stated critical standpoint, allowing the reader the knowledge of their own particular approaches from which their views may in turn be evaluated. The series therein hopes to introduce and to elucidate criticism of authors and texts being studied and to encourage participation as the critics debate.

Michael Scott

Acknowledgements

A book of this nature is primarily indebted to all the materials, and more, assembled in the bibliography and references section. However, a special acknowledgement must be made to Brian Vickers for his editorship of all the Shakespeare volumes in the Critical Heritage series. The inter-library loan staff of the University of Reading library are thanked for their patience and efficiency. Michael Scott, the general editor of the series, is thanked for his advice and Lilian Argrave for her typing skills. Throughout the preparation and writing of the volume my colleague Andrew Gurr generously contributed his bibliographical knowledge of the subject and kindly gave me some references from research, while Raymond Powell helped keep me abreast of contemporary criticism.

Finally, I would like to dedicate this study to a former colleague whose friendship, learning, inspiration and laughter, are sorely missed.

In Memoriam
Ian Fletcher
1920–1988

Preface

THIS BOOK is neither an annotated bibliography nor a history of the criticism of *Henry IV Parts I & II*. It is hoped that the major landmarks in discussion of the plays have received some attention, though only a tip of the periodical iceberg has been touched upon. While some criticism has become redundant, not all worthwhile studies could be included within the scope of this work. In researching the material a criterion for most selections emerged of itself. Works most commonly referred to by successive critics, scholars and teachers became the focus of the study. The exception is Hermann Ulrici who, as far as I am aware, has been resurrected from undeserved nineteenth-century oblivion and given credit here for his critical prescience.

There are several ways in which this book may be used: read through from cover to cover, or dipped into according to its historical divisions. A reader only interested in more modern commentary can turn directly to that section. Alternatively, anyone wishing to follow up whatever is said about a particular critic on *Henry IV Parts I & II* can work from the index. The 'Bibliographies, Guides and Surveys' section provides references for those who wish to explore discussion of the interrelationship of all of Shakespeare's English history plays. Full details of authors and works referred to in the text are found in the 'References' section.

The texts referred to throughout this study are those of A. R. Humphreys in the Arden Shakespeare (*Part I*, 1960; *Part II*, 1966).

Part One: Survey

The seventeenth century

Henry IV Part I along with *Richard III* was the most published of Shakespeare's plays in the seventeenth century, and although *Othello* appears to have been the most popular play, references to Falstaff throughout the century were so numerous as to be unrivalled in Shakespeare's, or any other dramatist's characters. Though Shakespeare's reputation grew in the last two decades of the seventeenth century evidence indicates that, overall, Ben Jonson's reputation was higher and that his *Catiline* (1614) was the most famous play of the century. But, nevertheless, Falstaff as a character reigned supreme. Occasional reference to Falstaff, Pistol, Doll, Shallow and Silence in *Part II* are found but the overwhelming majority of references are to Falstaff in *Henry IV Part I*. Falstaff was remembered for his girth, drinking, wit and buffoonery – particularly in relation to the Gadshill exploit. Several references defend the reputation of Sir John Oldcastle, the Lollard martyr whom Falstaff was originally named after. It is believed that the portrayal gave offence to Oldcastle's influential descendants and Shakespeare prudently altered the name. The dominance of *Henry IV Part I* and consequent underestimation of *Henry IV Part II* can be seen most strikingly in what is known as the Dering Manuscript. This document, the earliest surviving manuscript of a Shakespeare play, is a composite of *Henry IV Parts I & II*. Sir Edward Dering slightly revised an existing abridgement, thought to have been made for court performance. The abridgement, dating from approximately 1613 consists of three-quarters of *Henry IV Part I*, including all of Falstaff's scenes, but only II.2 of *Henry IV Part II* with Falstaff and Mistress Quickly, and a truncated rejection scene. The Gloucester scenes are cut and little is seen of the Lord Chief Justice, the rebels, or the Archbishop. That is, the Dering Manuscript's presentation of Falstaff corresponds closely to the recorded allusions to the fat knight throughout the seventeenth century. This composite anticipates twentieth-century arguments concerning structure, and stresses the Hal regeneration plot at the expense of the increased complexity of Falstaff's character which Shakespeare developed in *Henry IV Part II*.

The first discussion of *Henry IV* by a major critic occurs in John Dryden's 'An Essay on Dramatic Poesie' (1668) and in 'The Grounds of Criticism in Tragedy' included in 'The Preface to Troilus and Cressida' (1679). Again, in both instances, it is Falstaff who is chosen to illustrate an argument. In the former Dryden considers the popular categorisation of Falstaff in terms of the comedy of humours whereby a distinguishing trait is not merely individual but part of an observable species of character and behaviour. For 'Others ... there are many men resembling [Falstaff]: old, fat, merry, cowardly, drunken, amorous, vain, and lying' (p.139). To Dryden this is comparable to the psychological and social stereotypes of New Comedy, the heritage of Menander (40 BC) and the Roman comedy of Plautus and Terence (20 BC), whereas Falstaff is something greater, 'he is not properly one humour, but a miscellany of humours ...' (p.140), and it is his wit which makes him singular. Dryden's awareness of the complexity of human character was greater than the compartmentalised prescriptions of French neoclassical theory which he felt bound to follow. Thus, in 'The Grounds of Criticism in Tragedy'

> it is still to be observed that one virtue, vice and passion ought to be shown in every man, as predominant over all the rest: as covetousness in Crassus, love of his country in Brutus; (p.258)

Yet in the same place he writes:

> A character, or that which distinguishes one man from all others, cannot be supposed to consist of one particular virtue, or vice, or passion only; but 'tis a composition of qualities which are not contrary to one another in the same person ... Falstaff is a liar, and a coward, and a glutton, and a buffoon, because all these qualities may agree in the same man. (pp.257–8)

Dryden senses that the conception of Falstaff is greater than the available critical terminology. On the other hand, for a younger contemporary, the clergyman critic Jeremy Collier, Falstaff's fate exemplified necessary artistic didacticism, the playwright exacting justice. 'The Poet was not so partial as to let his Humour compound for his Lewdness' and Falstaff 'is thrown out of Favour as being a *Rake*, and dies like a rat behind the Hangings' (p.88). And such was to be the fate of *Henry IV Parts I & II* and its main characters, Hal, King Henry, Hotspur and Falstaff, all running the critical gamut from sympathy to hostility, thereafter.

The eighteenth century

The problem of *Henry IV Parts I & II* for eighteenth-century critics generally was Falstaff and the relationship between his wit and humour and his evident vices. Was the former to be enjoyed and the latter decried? That is, were these things to be separated? If not, how did one affect the other? Does the comedy subsume morality or vice versa? Linked to the question of Falstaff's vices was the issue of the rejection at the close of *Henry IV Part II* and the character of Hal, or Henry V as he is at the point of rejection. Hal's morality and the political behaviour of the Lancastrians, which becomes a major issue of criticism by the mid twentieth century, begins in the eighteenth century in a small but pointed fashion, the appearance in the second half of the eighteenth century of a sense of shock at John of Lancaster's machiavellian betrayal of his word at Gaultree Forest, and the summary execution of the rebel leaders.

At the outset of the century in what was to remain an influential edition of Shakespeare's works, Nicholas Rowe in his preface raised the crucial issues that were to remain foremost in eighteenth-century critical debate. Praising Falstaff as a masterpiece he writes:

> If there be any Fault in the Draught he has made of this lewd old Fellow, it is that tho' he has made him a Thief, Lying, Cowardly, Vain-glorious, and in short every way Vicious, yet he has given him so much Wit as to make him almost too agreeable. (p.195)

Having engaged us with almost a paradox his own bias comes out strongly enough in what follows:

> and I don't know whether some people have not, in remembrance of the Diversion he had formerly afforded 'em, been sorry to see

his Friend *Hal* use him so scurvily when he comes to the Crown at the End of the Second Part of Henry IV. (p.195)

Without particularly stressing it, Rowe is quite aware of the power of performance. Though his qualm appears perhaps rather simple, it derives from something which many of his successors neglect. Falstaff's behaviour, as we shall see, is often seen in abstract moral terms. Abstract, that is, in the sense in which it is separated from the dramatic content, and seen non-dramatically as a moral issue calling for straightforward judgement. The 'fault' Rowe questions suggests something contrary, the imbalance between Shakespeare's exuberant dramatic complexity and the narrow confines of neo-classicism with its conventional distributive justice. Few following Rowe could take up the challenge he suggests, that comedy and morality, art and life in dramatic representation, are too complex for mere didacticism.

One way round the problem was simply to choose to ignore the questionable side of Falstaff's behaviour, or to see Falstaff as a kind of Jekyll and Hyde:

As to the Character of Sir *John Falstaff*, it is chiefly extracted from *Shakespeare*, in his *1st Part of King Henry the IVth*. But so far as *Sir John* in *Shakespeare's* Description sinks into a *Cheat* or a *Scoundrel* upon any Occasion, he is different from that *Falstaff* who is designed in the following *Essay*, and is entirely an amiable Character. (p.122)

This is the remarkable premise of Corbyn Morris's discussion of Falstaff in his examination of forms of comedy, namely 'Wit, Humour, Raillery, Satire and Ridicule'. Not only is age, sickness and disease in Falstaff's portrayal ignored in *Henry IV Part II*, and indeed throughout the play, but such a crucial action as Falstaff's stabbing the dead Hotspur in *Part I* is silently overlooked. For Morris Falstaff's fate in *Henry IV Part II* was 'written ... in compliance with the Austerity of the Times: and in order to avoid the Imputation of encouraging Idleness and mirthful Riot by too amiable and happy an example' (p.122). The powerful strain of benevolism and optimism that colours much eighteenth-century life and literature is evident in Morris's view of Humour as a natural and endearing whimsy or foible which touches the heart with sympathy. Wit, on the other hand, is an intellectual 'stroke of Art' at home in satire and raillery. Humour is part of feeling, wit of thought. The wit is superior to us, we feel superior to the humourist but are drawn sympathetically to him by reciprocal 'generous benevolent Sentiments of Heart' (p.123). However, the most accomplished artistic creations combine both, and this is the case with Falstaff, 'The *Ground-work is Humour*, or the Representation and Detection of a bragging and vaunting *Coward* in *real Life*' (p.124). This alone would have made the knight ultimately an object of derision, but 'here the inimitable *Wit* of *Sir John* comes in to his Support, and gives a new *Rise* and *Lustre* to his Character' (p.124). From this recognition Morris finds an acceptable resolution of the moral issue, 'for the sake of his wit you forgive his *Cowardice*; or rather, are fond of his *Cowardice* for the Occasions it gives to his *Wit*' (p.124). Evidently 'fondness' mollifies censure and the genteel Sir John's '*jovial* and *gay* Humour, without any thing *envious, malicious, mischievous*, or *despicable*, and continually *quicken'd* and adorn'd with *Wit*, yields . . . peculiar *Delight*, without any *Alloy*' (p.126). But that stabbing remains to trouble the reader and the 'alloy' is arguably the quality that makes for the very complexity and richness of Falstaff.

Later in the century Richard Cumberland gave a similar view, 'His lies, his vanity and his cowardice, too gross to deceive, were to be so ingenious as to give delight' (p.457). Only someone so unique, he claims, could tempt royalty, a view often found elsewhere. Others felt that in Falstaff vice and laughter must be separated. According to Arthur Murphy,

> His wit and, on all Occasions, the Pleasantry of his ideas provokes us to laugh with him, and hinder the knight's character from sinking into contempt; and we love him, in Spight of his degrading Foibles. (p.257)

This asks for a peculiarly divided response in which the comic subsumes the moral, whereas Elizabeth Griffith, in her avowedly moral study of Shakespeare's plays, moral in the sense that all of Shakespeare is extensively gleaned as a compendium of moral edification, considering the character of Falstaff finds

> I was obliged to pass by many of his strokes of humour, character, and description . . . but I honestly confess that it was with regret

> whenever I did so; for were there are as much moral, as there
> certainly is physical good in laughing, I might have transcribed
> every Scene of his . . . (pp.139–40)

The laughter of comedy is seen as a physical thing only and its
'goodness' as something separate from moral good. Mrs Griffith
never questions for a moment the double standard here, but at least
she allows the conundrum to remain whereas for Henry Mackenzie
reaction to Falstaff took the form of two simultaneously opposed
modes in both the audience and Hal

> The audience . . . were to be in the same predicament as the
> Prince, to laugh and admire while they despised. To feel the
> power of his humour, the attraction of his wit, the justice of his
> reflections, while their contempt and their hatred attended the
> lowness of his manners, the grossness of his pleasures, and the
> unworthiness of his vice. (p.441)

In some respects Mackenzie's stress on imagination in reading
Shakespeare and the nature of originality in character anticipates
romantic responses, but earlier in the century William Guthrie's
rejection of the influence of French neoclassicism gave voice to a
view that was eventually to triumph in romanticism.

Neoclassical critics, the most formidable of whom were Thomas
Rymer and John Dennis, censured Shakespeare according to the
prescriptive 'rules' of art inherited principally from Aristotle and
Homer. Shakespeare, it was considered, did not observe the classical
unities of time, place and action. Further, he mixed the hetero-
geneous subjects of tragedy and comedy. His language was riddled
with puns and bombast with a distasteful admixture of 'low terms'.
Shakespeare did not follow imitation, in the sense that, for neo-
classicism, imitation of nature was actually closer to imitation of art.
The art which embodied nature was the literature of the past, above
all of Homer, and it was considered that the essence of this imitation
and nature was the idealised type – what men should be rather than
what men are. Not only did Shakespeare give us the raw, observable
passions of man, his actual behaviour ('manners') but he also
neglected necessary didacticism and poetic justice. Shakespeare was
not 'correct'.

A blanket defence was that the so-called faults of Shakespeare

were in fact the faults of an unrefined age. More specifically, anti-
neoclassical critics turned against the insistence on the unities and
claimed that the mixture of tragedy and comedy created something
great, comparable to the epic. Moreover, in terms that anticipate
romanticism, Shakespeare's irregularities were considered not a
limitation, but part of his noble genius, a genius greater for its
apparent lack of learning, and thus unfettered by imitation, rule and
prescription. In short the nature of Shakespeare's genius was *above*
art. And returning to Guthrie we find one of the most striking
statements of the eighteenth century, recalling Vasari's praise of
Michelangelo, to this effect:

> It is not Shakespeare who speaks the language of nature, but
> nature rather speaks the language of Shakespeare. He is not so
> much her imitator as her master, her director, her moulder.
> (pp.194–5)

Caliban in *The Tempest* is given as an example of this, and then the
more complex instance of the tragedy of Othello and Desdemona.
Their love would seem unlikely and unnatural, and compassion for a
vile murderer would seem out of the question. Yet Shakespeare's
genius gives us nature, compassion and tears. Guthrie's third
example is Falstaff:

> Nature never designed that a complication of the meanest, the
> most infamous, the most execrable qualities should form so
> agreeable a composition, that we think Henry the fifth makes a
> conquest of himself when he discards Jack Falstaff. Yet Shake-
> speare has struck out this moral contradiction, and reconciled it to
> nature. There is not a spectator who does not wish to drink a cup
> of sack with the merry mortal, and who does not in his humour
> forget, nay sometimes love his vices. (p.195)

Though a 'moral contradiction', Falstaff's virtues and vices are not
self-cancelling. The balance falls on humour and the sentimentalist
ethic subsumes vice. This, to the moralist, was the gravest of
dangers and needed to be clearly seen as such. Accordingly, the
greatest moralist and critic of the eighteenth century took his stand
and Dr Johnson weighed the beefy knight against the gravity of his
own uncompromising morality.

In his famous 'Preface to Shakespeare' Dr Johnson roundly trounces the neoclassicists in celebrated passages, but it is in an end-note to *Henry IV Part II* in his edition of the works of Shakespeare that he turns to Falstaff. Taking an epithet which had become attached to Falstaff Dr Johnson asks 'But *Falstaff* unimitated, unimitable *Falstaff*, how should I describe thee?' The epideictic flourish with the rhetorical question following the laudatory epithets makes the measured severity of all that follows even more damning. 'Falstaff is a character loaded with faults, and with those faults which naturally produce contempt' (p.124). He is a thief, glutton, coward and boaster who exploits the weak, poor and defenceless: he is patronising and obsequious, opinionated and deceitful. In all, he is corrupt and despicable. What then of the celebrated wit and humour? Dr Johnson recognises this, but in such a way that goes against most of those critics mentioned above. Falstaff's 'perpetual gaiety' and 'unfailing power of exciting laughter' is acknowledged. Dr Johnson even goes so far to admit that as Falstaff is not guilty of any great crime his humour lessens the sense of offence, but his summary is unequivocal.

> The moral to be drawn from this representation is that no man is more dangerous than he that with a will to corrupt hath the power to please; and that neither wit nor honesty ought to think themselves safe with such a companion when they see *Henry* seduced by *Falstaff*. (pp.124–5)

The whirligig of time brings in many reversals, as well as revenges, and no one could have quite predicted the extreme case that was put forward some ten years after Dr Johnson, which argued that not only was Falstaff not a coward, but he was a man of courage. This claim was extensively argued in the most famous study of the eighteenth century, *An Essay on the Dramatic Character of Falstaff* (1777) by Maurice Morgann. The critics' debate thus far, as we have seen, concentrates on Falstaff and focuses on the relationship of morality and comedy, wit and vice. Morgann's controversial move was to go to the root of the morality issue and argue against Falstaff's cowardice.

Commentators on Morgann's *Essay* usually begin, as he does, with some account of the theoretical framework, namely the concepts of 'Impression' and 'Understanding'. As if the thesis was not paradoxical enough in itself, Morgann exaggerates the mode at the outset by reversing the common meaning of these terms. 'Understanding' is rather superficial – inferring motive and character from a person's actions only. Thus Falstaff's behaviour at Gadshill and Shrewsbury seems that of a coward. Impressions are more complex, 'first principles of character', something more consistently enduring that lies beneath action. Our intuition informs us of this, however contradictory it might appear. Elsewhere Morgann refers more simply to appearance and reality. For all the seeming sophistication and refinement, part of Morgann's position is very much that of many of his predecessors; that is, it is simply not adequate to say Falstaff is a coward. The wit and humour has to be taken into account, and here Morgann seems to have a strong point; 'Laughter and approbation attend his greatest excesses; and being governed visibly by no settled bad principle or ill design, fun and humour account for and cover all' (p.167). But is not this as limited and naive as the opposed views he is reacting against? Only one page of the *Essay* touches on *Henry IV Part II*, conceding the moral decline of Falstaff just before the rejection. The issues of age, sickness and death, the noted sombreness of *Henry IV Part II*, is ignored. However, the comedy of Falstaff is not the main thrust of his argument.

From a strong impression, the reverse of common understanding, Morgann hypothesises 'constitutional courage' (p.176). Not courage according to the prevailing chivalric code of honour (Falstaff is clearly deficient in this), but 'Natural courage'. The plainest explanation of this, according to Morgann, is that Falstaff is never really fearful (Morgann will not accept the bellowing at Gadshill). Indeed, at Shrewsbury, this 'military freethinker' shows a resoluteness of words and actions in avoiding death against the superior Douglas. However, with the discussion of the wit of Falstaff's 'counterfeit' stratagem here, we are forced into the droll equation that constitutional courage equals the preservation of wit. Not so much discretion is the better part of valour as wit is the better part of courage! For evidence of courage Morgann makes questionable biographical inferences and accepts any internal estimation of Falstaff without allowing for the role of character and the function of irony. For instance, Coleville's surrender (*Henry IV Part II*, IV.3) is seen as an acknowledgement of Falstaff's valour without any sense of how structurally the purpose of the scene is to reflect on the preceding one. Falstaff's valour is as bogus as John of Lancaster's honour at Gaultree; he is not the vanquisher of Hotspur as Coleville obviously believes. To discredit those who malign Falstaff Morgann has to distort character so much that, for example, Poins, the deeply malicious rival in his pages, is quite unrecognisable as Shakespeare's character. At times, Morgann is very responsive to the comedy as when Falstaff enters the Boar's Head tavern after Gadshill with 'A plague of all cowards, I say' (*Henry IV Part I*, II.4.3). Rightly here Morgann insists on recognising the effect on an audience, the comic undercutting the moral. But elsewhere he drops any comic response and accepts Falstaff on his own terms, again without recognition of the irony at work, as when Falstaff claims he used 'the utmost speed in his power' to catch up with the army. When eventually he has to confront Gadshill, Morgann claims it is a 'single instance' (p.176) only, and as for the stabbing of the dead Hotspur, this is considered 'indecent but not cowardly' (p.175). Most glaring of all, perhaps, is Morgann's insistence that Falstaff as vanquisher of Hotspur did not intend to impose on anyone which goes flatly against his subsequent behaviour and Hal's immediate reply, 'If a lie may do thee grace . . .' (*Henry IV Part I*, V.4.156). For the most part Morgann hypostatises the character of Falstaff, removing him from the given artistic context and conferring on him a historical reality.

Richard Stack, Morgann's most powerful critic, remarked that dramatic characters are 'not drawn for speculative ingenious men in their closets, but for mankind at large' (p.475). But there was a good reason for Morgann's rarefied Falstaff of the study, which he alludes to in the *Essay* when he embarks on a contemptuous aside on the farcical vulgarisation of the actors of Falstaff, particularly when counterfeiting death at Shrewsbury and exaggerating cowardice. Morgann's account appears to be derived from actual performance and it is worth quoting at length for an evocation of the eighteenth-century stage. Falstaff's cowardice, then

is also aggravated to the spectators by the idle tricks of the Player, who practises on this occasion all the attitudes and wild apprehensions of fear; more ambitious, as it should seem, of representing a Caliban than a *Falstaff*; or indeed rather a poor unwieldy miserable Tortoise than either. – The painful Comedian lies spread out on his belly, and not only covers himself all over with his robe as with a shell, but forms a kind of round Tortoise-back by I know not what stuffing or contrivance; in addition to which, he alternately lifts up, and depresses, and dodges his head, and looks to one side and to the other, so much with the piteous aspect of that animal, that one would not be sorry to see the ambitious imitator calipashed in his robe, and served up for the entertainment of the gallery. (Fineman's edition, p.154)

In spite of three distinguished Falstaffs in the eighteenth century, namely those of Francis Betterton, James Quinn and John Henderson, it appears that Falstaff was often played for laughter only. Evidence indicates that Betterton avoided excesses of salaciousness and crude farce. Quinn was highly praised in his day, particularly by Lord Lyttleton, 'such perfection . . . he was not an actor . . . he was *Falstaff* himself!' (p.412). Laughter, too much of it for Henry Mackenzie, characterised Henderson's portrayal, 'He exchanged the comic gravity of the old school' as Arthur Colby Sprague records (p.55) and he was criticised for his visible manifestation of cowardly fear in a review influenced by Morgann. However, the farcical element Morgann criticised was nowhere more brought out than in the legacy of Shakespeare's stage direction '*He takes up Hotspur on his back*' (*Henry IV Part I*, V.4.128). Quinn had managed this, though not without audience laughter, but Henderson had great difficulty and had to settle for some of his attendant recruits to do the job. Francis Gentleman dismissed all this as 'pantomime mummery' (p.94), and clearly to someone of Morgann's sensibility it was not only demeaning but went entirely against the psychological reading of Falstaff he was propounding, albeit paradoxically.

However, perhaps Morgann has been fundamentally misunderstood? At one point he remarks 'But I have here raised so much new matter, that the reader may be out of hope of seeing this argument, any more than the tale of *Tristram*, brought to a conclusion' (Fineman, p.207). Morgann's *Essay* was written some seven years after Laurence Sterne's celebrated comic novel *The Life and Opinions of Tristram Shandy Gentleman*. In this the learned Mr Shandy, father of Tristram, takes delight in the recondite, pedantic and paradoxical in evidence and argument. (At one point, Mr Shandy is engrossed by a legal argument 'That the mother is not of kin to her child'.) Morgann alludes playfully to the 'critical amusement' he is providing in which he hopes the reader will excuse him from 'the

strict severity of logical investigation' (Fineman, p.163). Both
Morgann and Sterne are following 'the tradition of learned wit', as it
has been called by D. W. Jefferson, comprising such figures as Swift,
Rabelais and Erasmus, in which dexterity of mind pursues the
whimsical, outrageous and indefensible as an exercise in wit, rather
than truth. Many have questioned the ultimate seriousness of
Morgann's intention but without recognising the provenance of the
literary mode. If this conjecture is true then Falstaff can be seen as a
stalking horse for his larger critical objective, '*Falstaff* is the word
only, Shakespeare is the *Theme*' (Fineman, p.163) Morgann tells us.
And indeed at one point Morgann digresses suggestively on Shakespeare's conception of character in terms of organic growth, culture
and environment. Though there were admirers of his main thesis,
Dr Johnson spoke for the majority when he speculated to Boswell
that Morgann would 'come forth again, and as he has proved
Falstaff to be no coward, he may prove Iago to be a very good
character' (IV, p.192).

For B. Walwyn the attribution of courage was simply inconsist-
ent. Though Morgann had stressed Falstaff's mirth Thomas Davies
pointed out 'that if the knight is proved to be a man of courage half
the mirth he raises is quite lost and misplaced' (p.373) and he saw
Falstaff's stabbing of Hotspur as a sure sign of cowardice. For all the
prevailing benevolism and optimism, even as late as 1788, William
Richardson could echo the harsh uncompromising moral view. For
him Falstaff is 'a mean sensualist forever depraved' (p.499). In the
same year Richard Stack provided the most well-known refutation of
Morgann.

Stack turns the theoretical tables on Morgann by arguing that the
'understanding' is much more comprehensive than is allowed for.
Instinctive 'impressions' could well mislead. Stack draws attention
to Shakespeare's obvious design in the first Boar's Head scene, going
through Morgann's points but strictly readapting them to Shakespeare's order of presentation, showing their partiality and weakness. With a muted wit of his own Stack argues that the first
impressions of Falstaff, so carefully designed by Shakespeare, are
true 'and any following appearances that may seem contradictory to
them I should incline to all errors of the understanding' (p.470).
Throughout Stack is commonsensical, restrained and polite, and not
responding to any Shandean play of wit, his restrained implication is
that Morgann has undergone a monstrously inflated self-deception.

The refutation is overwhelming in particular and general. One line demolishes Morgann's defence of the stabbing of Hotspur – 'is it possible for such an idea to enter into the mind of a brave man?' (p.477). Stack's Falstaff aligns him with one of the main lines of critical argument we have looked at so far, 'in the gay wit we forget the contemptible coward' (p.479). In addition Stack notes particularly Shakespeare's 'exquisite contrivance . . . in catching occasion of mirth from [Falstaff's] very vices' (p.479). Stack is very enjoyable to read and plain common sense always has a weighty persuasiveness at least up to that point when we feel some qualm about simply dismissing Morgann. At the heart of his *Essay*, in spite of inconsistencies (he repeatedly reverts to Falstaff as a buffoon), he is attempting to respond to his feelings which react to a more profound complexity in Falstaff than his contemporaries allowed for, and it was this legacy which was taken up at the beginning of the twentieth century, by no less a figure than A. C. Bradley. Falstaff dominates critical discussion of *Henry IV Parts I & II* in the seventeenth and eighteenth centuries so much so that very little else of any substance is remarked upon, apart from the character of Hal and the conduct of Prince John at Gaultree Forest.

Rowe's easy-going liberalism saw Falstaff at the rejection as 'scurvily' treated by Hal. Towards the end of the century Richardson records 'Persons of eminent worth feel for [Falstaff] some attachment, and think him hardly used by the king' (p.499). But there are few such persons on record. Recognising Hal's 'repugnance and self-consideration' as he matures 'towards a thorough reformation', Cumberland nevertheless feels the 'weakness of pity' (p.459) at the rejection. We are prepared for the change in Hal but not for Falstaff's fate. The sympathies of Rowe and Cumberland are exceptional and although they anticipate a major critical standpoint of the twentieth century, most eighteenth-century commentators ultimately sided with Hal, even if grudgingly.

William Guthrie, acknowledging Falstaff's faults nevertheless found him 'so agreeable a composition, that we think Henry the fifth makes a conquest of himself when he discards Jack Falstaff' (p.195). Richardson probably had Cumberland, his contemporary, in mind, finding that 'such feeling [attachment] is delusive, and arises from partial views' (p.499). Hal in his view is objectively self-aware of Falstaff's parasitism, and is not taken in. It is Falstaff who deceives himself while Hal is a man of 'discernment' who acts with 'humanity'.

In the twentieth century Hal's character, his 'reformation' and the rejection are major issues of debate. For the eighteenth century it was relatively uncomplicated. Warburton's contribution to Theobald's edition of Shakespeare provides an extended example. Given the rule of psychological consistency in character portrayal rather than improbable moral reversal, the audience is prepared for and expects the Prince's transformation.

> Sparks of innate Honour and true Nobleness break from him upon every proper Occasion where we would hope to see him awake to Sentiments suiting his birth and Dignity. (p.479)

Above all, Warburton points out, Shakespeare has ensured our anticipation in the famous soliloquy of *Henry IV Part I*, I.2, 'I know you all ...' Almost inevitably, when the question of morality, character and literature arises it is Dr Johnson to whom we turn. In considering the same soliloquy, Dr Johnson's greater impartiality finds a psychological insight, not just a rhetorical signal.

> This speech is very artfully introduced to keep the Prince from appearing vile in the opinion of the audience; It prepares them for his future reformation, and, in what is yet more valuable, exhibits a natural picture of a great mind offering excuses to itself, and palliating those follies which it can neither justify nor forsake. (p.118)

Greatness for Dr Johnson lies in the realisation of human fallibility, not in the presentation of idealised types according to neoclassical decorum. Thus in Prince Hal 'the trifler is roused into a hero, and the hero again reposes into a trifler. This character is great, original and just' (p.124). On the other hand Elizabeth Montagu finds a paradoxical decorum in apparent indecorousness. Hal's youthful excesses would have been unduly magnified 'if they had appeared in a piece entirely serious and full of dignity and decorum' (p.332). Fortunately, Falstaff's seductive humour provides amoral justification and probability in its psychological attractiveness for the Prince, in a kind of counter-decorum. With Hal's brother, Prince John, antipathy rather than sympathy has marked critical response both then and now.

In *Henry IV Part II*, IV.2, Westmoreland and Prince John parley with the principle rebels, the Archbishop of York, Mowbray and Hastings who present their grievances which Prince John promises will be redressed:

> I like them all, and do allow them well,
> And swear here, by the honour of my blood,
> My father's purposes have been mistook,
> And some about him have too lavishly
> Wrested his meaning and authority.
> My Lord, these griefs shall be with speed redress'd.

(ll.54–9)

The Archbishop's acknowledgement has a stress which Prince John's rejoinder emphasises.

> *Arch.* I take your princely word for these redresses.
> *Lanc.* I give it to you, and will maintain my word.

(ll.66–7)

When the rebels' army is disbanded they are promptly arrested, charged with high treason and summarily executed. Mowbray's protest 'Is this proceeding just and honourable?' (l.110) bothers the critics more than it does Prince John who replies,

> I pawn'd thee none.
> I promised you redress of these same grievances
> Whereof you did complain; which, by mine honour,
> I will perform with a most Christian care.

(ll.113–15)

Several of the terms here are crucial for *Henry IV Parts I & II* as a whole as will be examined in the Appraisal section later, suffice it here to note the conscious cynicism which separates the grievances from those who made them. 'Christian care' becomes machiavellian duplicity.

One important point should be stressed here. Benjamin Heath remarked 'This whole proceeding, as it is represented by the poet, is founded in strict historical truth' (p.557). This is not true. In the

Chronicles it was Westmoreland who did the treatying. Prince John at sixteen was too young. Shakespeare chose to adjust this and focus political duplicity on a representative of the house of Lancaster. Heath continues:

> It hath however a very unhappy and disagreeable effect on the reader or spectator, as instead of acquiescence at least in the punishment of the rebels it cannot fail of exciting in him compassion towards them when so treacherously ensnared, as well as a very high degree of indignation against Prince John, who is on all other occasions represented as a Prince of great gallantry and magnanimity, for prostituting his character by so deliberate and odious a piece of perfidy. (p.557)

We might wish to question the uniformity of the portrayal of Prince John suggested here, but otherwise this was how Gaultree was seen in the eighteenth century. In the same year as Heath, Dr Johnson felt that 'this horrible violation of faith' raised 'indignation' when 'passed over thus slightly by the poet, without any note of censure or detestation' (p.122). This was the issue, not so much the betrayal itself, but the fact that it was not condemned by Shakespeare: 'I wish [Shakespeare] had employed his eloquence ... in arraigning the baseness and treachery of John of Lancaster's conduct in breaking his covenant with the rebels' (p.334), said Elizabeth Montagu. Thomas Davies compares the Chronicles, but without noting the altered roles of Westmoreland and Prince John, otherwise commenting on Shakespeare's fidelity in 'This masterpiece of infamous treachery and breach of compact' (p.374) uncensured by both the Chronicles and Shakespeare. Just one critic sees a possible reason (or is it rationalisation?) of the betrayal. Edward Capell suggests that the political doctrine of passive obedience, by which in no circumstances did any subject have the right of resistance to a monarch, might account for Gaultree.

> Blameable as this behaviour will seem at this time of day, no disapprobation is shown of it by the historians that Shakespeare follow'd, which historians (it should be noted) were his contemporaries, the passive-obedience doctrine running so high with them that all proceedings with rebels were reckon'd justifiable. (p.559)

The nineteenth century

Whereas the character of Falstaff dominated eighteenth-century criticism, in the nineteenth century *Henry IV Parts I & II* came to be regarded as a gallery of characters. That is, Falstaff takes his place beside Hal and Hotspur principally, as these in turn are seen against their varying associates and backgrounds. This inevitably contrasted pair are mostly seen in idealised terms, although in the course of the century Shakespeare's somewhat dualistic view of both is recognised and indeed a distinctly anti-Lancastrian criticism begins to emerge. To some extent the heritage of Morgann is felt in the way that the plays came to be regarded as alternative fictions, and we find the development of the critic as a kind of omniscient narrator 'reading' plays as though he were a novelist creating characters. Perhaps the most notorious extreme of this is Mary Cowden Clarke's *The Girlhood of Shakespeare's Heroines* (1850–52) in which the detail of Shakespeare's characters is taken as a retrospective point of departure for an imaginative biographical reverie (the treatment of one historical personage, Lady Macbeth, begins with her birth!). More fruitfully, in other criticism, determinants of character are eventually discussed as thematic projections providing a critical focus and a principle of dramatic unity. Here the question of honour is paramount.

One critic, as we shall see, stands apart in the nineteenth century. Hermann Ulrici's comments on *Henry IV Parts I & II* had little influence then, or after, but in fact they anticipate much of the post-war modernist approach. Ulrici was a hundred years ahead of his time. Coming from the tradition of German thought which fostered Karl Marx, Ulrici's tempered Hegelianism provides a historicist grasp of Shakespeare's portrayal of the contradictions of feudal society. Instead of falling in with any post-Morgann discussion of character, he boldly perceives Shakespeare's structured contrast of character and milieu for critically parodic purposes, ably placing the function of comedy as diagnostic and subversive.

Jonathan Bate has shown the development in the late eighteenth century of the use of Shakespeare for political caricature and to establish an English school of history painting, perhaps best remembered by something like Reynolds' painting *Death of Cardinal Beaufort*, exhibited along with work by Northcote and Barry in John Boydell's Shakespeare Gallery in Pall Mall. However, a parallel development in literary criticism can be seen in the subtitle to William Maginn's *Shakespearean Papers* (1859), 'Pictures Grave and Gay' wherein Falstaff is selected to begin a series of 'portraits'. Portrait is H. N. Hudson's actual term when he summarises Shakespeare's portrayal of King Henry, 'taking the whole delineation together, we have at full length and done to the life, the portrait of a man in act prompt, bold, decisive . . .' (p.70). Again with 'the portrait of Glendower' (p.77) the analogy between portrait gallery and play is plain. However, celebrated stage performances of Falstaff like that of Kemble still encouraged criticism devoted to the fat knight and that is what is found in two of the greatest Romantic critics with strongly contrasted views, Coleridge and Hazlitt. John Payne Collier recorded in his diary Coleridge's view that as a character of 'complete moral depravity' (p.30) Falstaff was to be aligned with Richard III and Iago. Coleridge's superfine Germanic intellectuality distinguishes between the condition of being depraved and the self-conscious willing of depravity. To maintain this view soliloquies and asides are not considered in terms of the development of theatrical conventions but as naturalist psychological expressions of Shakespeare's satanic puppeteers. In contrast Hazlitt's fundamental premise is that Falstaff is a 'comic character . . . an actor in himself as much as upon the stage' (p.118). Whereas Coleridge silently discounts the theatrical, Hazlitt makes it the basis of his essential discrimination, 'we no more object to the character of Falstaff in a moral point of view than we should think of bringing an excellent comedian, who should represent him to the life, before one of the police officers' (pp.118–19). Hazlitt recognises a comic mode of theatrical representation as against unequivocal immorality in life itself. Implicit, though unexplored, in his comment, is the awareness that each requires a separate mode of value judgement. Though J. M. Robertson towards the end of the century insisted that Falstaff and his cohorts 'have a roundness of comic reality [which] remains comic reality' (p.155) it is not until debates of the early twentieth century that the critical view of Falstaff moves from character to theatrical typologies. Before that, however, we need to recognise the development of the critic as omniscient narrator.

In many respects Morgann provided a precedent for this, but in more general terms the rise of the novel and its prominence as the dominant literary form in the nineteenth century influenced the way critics read and responded to drama. Consider the following examples.

THE NINETEENTH CENTURY   31

[Falstaff] grumbles not at the advancement of men of his own order; but the bitter drop of his soul overflows when he remembers how he and that cheeseparing Shallow began the world, and reflects that the starveling justice has land and beeves, while he, the wit and the gentleman, is penniless, and living from hand to mouth by the casual shifts of the day. (Maginn, p.45)

Henry has it at least to preserve the royal honour he has acquired to himself and to his house; an ardent love of honour urges him to maintain himself in this position in spotless esteem; it grieves him, therefore, that his son should threaten to forfeit this honour by his unbridled conduct. All that in his own reputation and life might darken its splendour, he seeks with a thousand arts to hide deep within his secret heart. (Gervinus, p.322)

The Prince entered heartily and without reserve into the fun and frolic of his Eastcheap life; the rigour and the folly of it were delightful; to be clapped on the back, and shouted for as 'Hal', was far better than the doffing of caps and crooking of knees, and delicate unreal phraseology of the court. (Dowden, p.211)

It must be said that these examples indicate an occasional tendency in these critics, but it is a tendency which reproduces the drama as historical romance or picaresque closer to Sir Walter Scott or Harriet Ainsworth than to Shakespeare. Barrett Wendell not only compares Shakespeare to Scott, but actually sees him as a forerunner of the genre.

The full vitality of [*Henry IV*'s] conception allies it rather to the novels of Walter Scott: chronicle-history though it be, it is at the same time our first, and by no means our last, example of historical fiction. (p.167)

The romance of chivalry was part of the widespread influence of medievalism on nineteenth-century culture, and a reflection of it can be seen in the way critics idealised Hal and Hotspur.

Hazlitt provides the most succinct example. For him Hal and Hotspur are 'the essence of chivalry' (p.134). No argument is given; it is stated as self-evident. For Hazlitt the word 'chivalry' radiates a nimbus of unambivalent values. Elsewhere, in spite of qualification, heroism remains; Hal's soliloquy and the rejection of Falstaff are simply not an issue for Schlegel. And in spite of his low life connections Hal remains 'All ... amiability and attractiveness' (p.424). Though Hotspur's rudeness, arrogance and obstinacy are noted, 'these errors ... cannot disfigure the majestic image of his noble youth.' (p.425) Again, Hudson confronts Hotspur's 'arrogant, domineering, capricious temper ... his bounding, sarcastic, overbearing Spirit' (p.782). And though 'irascible, headstrong' and 'impatient', yet 'chivalry reigns ... supremely' amongst the rebel war-chiefs. This is claimed without any sense of irony in the provocative combination of rebellion and chivalry. Even at Shrewsbury where 'if not perversely wrong-headed, he is so headstrong, peremptory, and confident even to rashness, as to be quite impracticable' (p.74), Hudson claims that, nevertheless 'he is never more truly the noble Hotspur than on this occasion' (p.74). But it is with Hal that Hudson's idealisation glows most blindingly. Here the criticism moves retroactively from the heroic Chronicle image of King Henry V and sees Hal bathed in this light. Consequently, for Hudson, he is 'the mirror of Christian princes ... the most finished gentleman as well as greatest statesman and best of men of his time' (pp.78–9). Where later critics were to find Lancastrian coldness, calculation, 'policy' and opportunism, Hudson's encomium trumpets 'tenderness of filial piety ... virtuous prudence ... magnanimity ... good nature ... chivalrous generosity ... modesty' (p.81), the last curiously at odds with the critic's own extravagance.

Similarly, one of the leading German commentators of the nineteenth century, G. G. Gervinus, at the outset of his portrait of Hotspur, claims that he is 'the ideal of all genuine and perfect manliness ... a model of genuine chivalry' (p.308). Yet Hotspur has jealousy and 'blind passion' (p.309) which cloud his military and political judgement. Though lack of self-control and arrogance are acknowledged, 'beyond this there is no ignoble vein in the man' (p.310). Furthermore, in reviewing the character Gervinus insists 'that honour lives and moves in this man' (p.310). Yet immediately following this he recognises that in Hotspur's ardour 'the means for this effacing of dishonour must heap new dishonour upon them, and that the motives are selfish' (p.311). Rebellion and the rehearsed division of the kingdom fired by 'ill-weaved ambition' – 'remains a blemish on his shield of honour, but the only one' (p.311). The romantic idealising premise of Gervinus's depiction precludes him from recognising an ambivalence made evident by the very facts he acknowledges. With the case of Hal, Gervinus makes any short-comings the leavening of 'the perfect essence of genuine humanity' (p.317). Though 'there might be some prudent calculation' and 'perhaps there is policy' (p.316), Hal is more comprehensively idealised since nothing can be redundant.

> For in this character the qualities of self-denial and self-mastery, the disdain of show, the resting upon that inmost hidden worth, the kernel of human existence, lie indeed expressed in his very faults. (p.320)

Alternatively, for Georg Brandes Hotspur is 'the hero of the feudal ages' (p.226). The omniscient author takes over as 'his hauberk clatters on his breast, his spurs jingle at his heel, wit flashes from his lips, while he moves and has his being in a golden nimbus of renown' (p.226). A feudal counterpart to Achilles, in Hotspur Shakespeare has depicted 'a master-type of manliness' (p.226). When Brandes gets to Hal it is not without some qualms. A comparison is drawn with the king as a 'shrewd, mistrustful and circumspect ruler' (p.234) whose policy was 'By being seldom seen, I could not stir/ But like a comet I was wonder'd at' (*Henry IV Part I*, III.2.46–7). For Brandes Hal adopts 'a scarcely less diplomatic policy' (p.234) in his soliloquy 'I know you all . . .'. Had he acted strictly according to it he would have been an 'unmitigated charlatan' (p.235). However, further consideration of Shakespeare's need to avoid any kind of miraculous transformation of character by apprising the spectator through the conventions of the soliloquy gives it sufficient justification. Consequently, even given the rejection, Brandes finds that in the last act Shakespeare endowed Hal with traits of 'irreproachable kingly magnanimity' (p.241).

Towards the end of the century in the criticism of F. S. Boas a firmer, more censorious view of Hotspur appears in a study that was part of the University Extension Manuals. While Boas recognises chivalric heroism, nevertheless he finds that 'Hotspur's honour is based upon a selfish principle' (p.266). And in considering the rebellion and proposed division of the Kingdom (*Henry IV Part I*, III.1). Boas allows a distinctly sardonic note to creep into his account

> this knightly Paladin does not scruple, for the sake of avenging private wrongs, to enter into a league with his countries hereditary

foes. He consents to see England broken up, and claims a third
share of the booty. (p.267)

What is remarkable about all nineteenth-century discussion of
Hotspur is the failure to recognise that for all the final seriousness of
his end and the significance of his political danger, he is a hugely
comic character – facetious, outrageous and provocative both as
character and comic performer, he is relished by the audience, then
and now. In the depiction of the later Middle Ages Boas finds that
Shakespeare 'laid bare the fatal flaw of the medieval system – its
glorification of individual "honour" and prowess at the expense of
national well-being' (pp.268–9). In contrast, on the whole Boas
praises Hal's portrayal, but it is praise tempered by reluctant scepticism. He finds that the rejection was a moral necessity but 'it seems
unpleasantly like the practical complement of his self-righteous
soliloquy in earlier days' (p.272). That troublesome soliloquy is seen
by Boas as a 'Pharisaical declaration [that] need not be taken too
literally' (p.270), but as an assuring aside for an audience. Later,
however, Vernon's celebrated report of 'the feathered mercury' and
those companions 'that daft the world aside' (*Henry IV Part I*,
IV.1.96) seems rather hard to accept given what we have seen up to
that point, 'a severely realistic criticism might even be tempted to
doubt whether the madcap of Eastcheap could be transformed in a
moment' (p.271). Again, with the King's 'death', Boas finds a hasty
'irreverence' in Hal's seizure of the crown and 'sophistry' in his plea
for pardon. It is such fissures in the idealised façade of Hal's
depiction which in just a few years, in another widely read study by
John Masefield in the Home University Library series, could open
up to an attack on Hal as 'remote and cold-blooded', 'a callous
young animal', 'quite common, quite selfish, quite without feeling'
(pp.112–13). In sum

> Prince Henry is not a hero, he is not a thinker, he is not even a
> friend; he is a common man whose incapacity for feeling enables
> him to change his habits whenever interest bids him. (p.112)

Masefield's view is asserted without argument or illustration and
clearly registers a deeply felt bias which extends to King Henry
himself: though, to Masefield he is 'the just, rather kind, man of
affairs who takes power' (p.110) in *Richard II*, in the later plays he

is 'a swollen, soured, bullying man, with all the ingratitude of a king and all the baseness of one who knows his cause to be wrong' (p.110).

However, 'that vile politician Bolingbroke' (*Henry IV Part I*, 1.3.238), Hotspur's resonant denunciation, certainly colours some twentieth-century views of the king, but the nineteenth-century view before Masefield was more mixed, seeing both attractive and unattractive sides of Henry. Gervinus almost echoes Hotspur with his view of the 'vile and corrupt policy and diplomacy of the king' (p.310) and though he is 'a prototype of diplomatic cunning' (p.302) yet he had a 'good side' (p.302) which shows kindness and compunction. With the plan for a crusade Henry shows both religious devotion and 'the most subtle political motives' (p.303). Though in one place 'a deeper dissembler' (p.307), elsewhere he is 'reserved, prudent' and 'circumspect' (p.306), a model of pragmatism, in fact.

Shakespeare's dualistic conception of character presentation is discussed later in the Appraisal section (Part Two) but H. N. Hudson responded to this mixed mode in a vocabulary with a kind of sliding scale of praise-censure topoi – 'sagacity', 'inscrutable', 'penetrating', 'bold', 'cold', 'sly', 'subtle' (pp.70–71). However, the balance falls strongly in favour of the king.

> though policy was the leading trait in this able man, nevertheless it was not so prominent but that other and better traits were strongly visible. And even in his policy there was much of the breadth and largeness which distinguish the statesman from the politician. Besides he was a man of prodigious spirit and carriage, had a real eye to the interests of his country as well as of his family, and in his wars he was humane much beyond the custom of his time. (p.71)

Though Swinburne took a less sympathetic view of Henry's 'self-interest' (p.112) as the principle of his pursuit of gain and commodity, Boas felt that this self-interest coincided with the interest of the country. Boas pays tribute to Henry's 'statecraft' in politics, his 'skill and resolution' in battle and his 'dauntless unwearied spirit' (p.263) in the face of necessity. Moreover, he goes so far as to descry 'a vein of tenderness deep down in that stern nature' (p.264). Yet within a few years, in an equally widely read book, Masefield could so soundly condemn the King and Hal. Curiously, the explanation seems to lie in the ambivalent critical attitude to Henry V since the 1890s.

Writing directly after the carnage of the First World War Gerald Gould offered a reading of *Henry V* as a comprehensive satire 'on monarchical government, on imperialism, on the baser kinds of "patriotism" and on war' (p.44). Henry V, 'the perfect hypocrite' (p.44) is consistent throughout the trilogy in his cunning opportunism deriving from the 'hereditary psychology' of the Lancasters. Though this harshness might be taken as a direct emotional response to the war, and possibly to post-Boer jingoist productions at Stratford, in fact Jorgensen (1) has shown its development in the 1890s.

W. B. Yeats and G. B. Shaw are the crucial figures here, but their objections were not unprecedented. As we would expect, Hazlitt's republican views predispose him against Henry V whose character he sees as directly following from that of Prince Hal, 'he was careless, dissolute and ambitious . . . His principles did not change with his situation and profession. His adventure on Gadshill was a prelude to the affair of Agincourt, only a bloodless one' (pp.125–6). Writing with the aestheticism of the 1890s behind him W. B. Yeats embroiders 'that sweet lovely rose' Richard II into a poet and martyr, a 'vessel of porcelain' in contrast to Henry V's 'vessel of clay', a man of 'gross vices' and 'coarse nerves' (p.108). In a notoriously memorable line G. B. Shaw accused Shakespeare of going through a 'worldly phase' in which he 'thrust such a Jingo hero as his Henry V down our throats' (p.426). In Shaw's review of a Haymarket production of *Henry IV Part I*, Hal's 'self-indulgent good-fellowship' is seen as 'consciously and deliberately treacherous', qualities of a young Philistine combining 'conventional propriety' with 'brute masterfulness' in public life with 'low-lived blackguardism' (p.426) in the private sphere – all a long way from the embodiment of chivalry and honour we have examined above.

In terms of thematic focus, where critics go beyond character study, the problem of honour is seen as central. In Gervinus's approach, study of the profundity of Shakespeare's portrayal of character takes us beyond mere 'political historical plays' to recognise 'true ethical dramas' with a 'moral centre of thought' (p.307). At the heart of the plays Gervinus finds a series of contrasted ideas of honour. For Henry honour is concerned with rank and position, something external and acquired which the wayward Hal seems to flout. If Henry is aware of social appearance Hal in contrast is preoccupied with self-esteem, 'he spiritualises and refines the idea of honour into the true dignity of man' (p.322). Though this rarefied notion might be seen in the newly crowned king at the end of *Part II*, Gervinus's critical clairvoyance glimpses it from the outset: 'the consciousness of this possession in himself is his consolation even through the appearance of business, and through the bad opinion of the world' (p.322). Though Hotspur's selfish motives had been observed earlier, Gervinus softens his résumé to a 'morbid thirst' for glory which is nevertheless based on 'noble pride', 'honourable feelings' and 'the bravest heart' (p.322). Of course Falstaff stands in contrast to all this. Here selfishness is transposed to the fat knight who 'seems utterly deprived of all sense of honour and shame' (p.322). Gervinus allows for the richness of the comedy in his assessment of Falstaff but essentially 'the very core or rather nullity of his nature' is his 'lack of honour' (p.327) made explicit in the famous 'catechism' of V.i.

George Brandes largely follows his immediate predecessor, Gervinus, by seeing the true nature of honour as forming 'the central theme of the whole play' (p.230), meaning dignity to the King, renown to Hotspur, the opposite of outward show to Hal, and 'nothingness' to Falstaff.

Standing apart from these critics on this approach to honour, and on most other views, is the genius of Hermann Ulrici. As a measure of Ulrici's achievement we can quickly mention Thomas Peregrine Courtenay's two volume *Commentaries on the Historical Plays of Shakespeare* of 1840, two years after Ulrici's study in German which was eventually published in English translation as *Shakespeare's Dramatic Art* in 1876. Courtenay's so-called *Commentaries* are a mishmash of historical anecdote and illustration from the chronicles with extensive quotation of the 'beauties' of Shakespeare. Any 'comment' as such is entirely uncritical. Turning to Ulrici we find the most comprehensive criticism of the century. Arguing against Gervinus and his followers, Ulrici questions the central emphasis given to the idea of honour, its contrasted representation in Hal and Hotspur, and its caricature in Falstaff. Apart from being narrow, one-sided and moralising, Ulrici feels that this approach does not account for the functions of many of the other characters, let alone the historical action itself. Even more radical is Ulrici's subordination of the dominant critical approach of the period – character study. For him characters certainly have psychological interest but more significantly these may be seen as 'living hieroglyphics' (p.236) of history, its motive and development. An Hegelian dynamism informs Ulrici's overview: the unity of historical drama consists not so much in the hero or action,

> It lies rather . . . in the unity of the *historical idea*, the motive of the historical movement, and thus in the unity of the character and the spirit of the age presented. (p.236)

Beginning with the king himself, Ulrici finds a conflict between the internal and the external. Internally, in terms of his character, Henry is fit to reign, but there is no real ethical base beyond the personal, that is in 'right' itself. Externally, whatever his gifts of character, the king has no legal outward right. He is *de facto* not *de jure* king, thus his contingent virtues lack the absolute formulation of right and justice. Consequently, the body politic of the state is unstable and civil war ensues. Here, Ulrici argues, Shakespeare dramatises the internal contradiction of the feudal state. What had been a personal relationship between vassals and king had become a legal relationship concerning landed estates. The collective estates of the feudal vassalry exceeded those of the king, and even one vassal could rival his feudal chief in material power. The arbitrary role of Richard II according to a theological view of kingship led to the usurpation not just of the monarch but of the idea of divine sanction itself. Conversely, the superior power of the great feudal barons inaugurated the struggle between the vassalry and the king which Henry was part of as Bolingbroke, and then victim of, as a king lacking external sanction. Ulrici''s major contribution is to see characters not just in terms of psychology or morality but as active parts of an hierarchic social structure which is collapsing inwardly because of a shift in the foundations of feudalism.

In *Henry IV Part I*, examining the chivalric aspect of feudalism, Ulrici finds a contradiction between the knight seeking personal honour and military glory, and the knight ensuring the welfare of the country and people. Clearly Hotspur's valour is aligned with this egotistical principle while Hal's conduct is appraised as 'the mind's conscious superiority over danger' (p.241). *Henry IV Part II* brings into focus the second side of feudalism, the spectacle of the great landowners forced to negotiate out of prudential political reasons as a 'semi-sovereign power' (p.242) representing thousands of dependents. This, to Ulrici, is the significance of the retainer Sir John Coleville in Act IV, scene iii. However, when Ulrici gets to Falstaff, the low-life scenes and the question of comedy, he is at his most incisive.

> . . . the Falstaff episode bears unmistakeably an ironical character; it is a parody on the historical representation . . . it is intended to parody the hollow pathos of political history . . . Irony is to hold up its concave mirror to that mere semblance of history . . . (p.244)

For Ulrici such things as rebellion, intrigues, war, victory, treaties, etc., are 'mere show, the mere mask of history' (p.244). Historicist idealism impels Ulrici to see a profounder reality in the underlying decay of justice and morality. Shakespeare's purpose in placing the comic scenes against the historical action was 'To give a clear exhibition of this morality, this semblance, this histrionic parade' (p.245). Examining Falstaff's role in the comic scenes Ulrici perceives the multi-faceted brilliance of Shakespeare's creation. Foremost, Falstaff is the 'personified parody' (p.245) on the corruption of chivalry and feudalism. The materialism of the baronial power-struggles are no less immoral than Falstaff's schemes and opportunism. Falstaff's boasting, bluster and bravado particularly parodies Hotspur, Douglas and Glendower. On the other hand his cautiousness, observations on war and politics, comments on life and death, and future existence, are again a distinct parody of Northumberland, Worcester and the bishop of York. Falstaff's mixture of assumed virtue and practical cunning parody the king himself. The comparisons of Falstaff serve to fill out the low-life milieu and thus provide a dramatic form of realism which makes Shakespeare's satirical intention less overt. In *Part II* the associates of Falstaff complete the picture and all contribute to the comedy which everywhere reflects in a pointed ironic fashion on the elements of the action in the main plot, history itself, in fact. Falstaff 'floats above the historical picture as its parodical image, explaining the significance of the actions and of the events represented' (p.246). Thus the Gadshill expedition is a 'withering travesty' on King Henry's relationship with the Percy faction in which the assumption and retention of the crown is seen as robbery and the defence of unlawfully acquired property.

Sometimes Ulrici takes the idea of parody too far, seeing it as almost all-encompassing, but he is right to stress something like Falstaff's appearance as the conqueror of Hotspur at the council of war after the battle of Shrewsbury as a parody of war, let alone his earlier business as the superior officer with his reunited cripples – a powerful indictment of the context of chivalry. More subtly, Ulrici presses home the point that Falstaff's wily dealings with the Hostess and the Lord Chief Justice parodies 'policy', the mainspring of the whole historical and dramatic action. Ultimately, for Ulrici, the meaning, purpose and value of real history lies in its manifestation of the ideal, ethically considered, in right and justice. Without this history has no real value. Shakespeare's purpose in adding the comic subplot to the chronicle material was to demonstrate that for all the surface action of affairs of state, history was empty and meaningless, the moral foundation broken and the organic equilibrium of the body politic disrupted and restless. The evident historicist principles here need not be completely accepted, but Ulrici's wide-ranging recognition of Shakespeare's dramatic engagement with and comic questioning of the intertwined personal and structural dynamics of history anticipates, as we shall see, some of the most challenging criticism of the twentieth century.

The twentieth century

Convention versus naturalism

The major critical debate of the early twentieth century was that of E. E. Stoll's objections to A. C. Bradley's published lecture of 1909, 'The Rejection of Falstaff'. It should be noted that when this appeared Bradley was recognised as the foremost Shakespeare critic of the day primarily because of the influence of his *Shakespearean Tragedy* (1904).

In the first part of the lecture Bradley points out that the rejection itself should not shock. If we had rightly responded to Shakespeare's presentation of Hal 'we should have been prepared for a display both of hardness and of policy at this point in his career' (p.254). Bradley acknowledges, in his view, an attractive side of Hal who eventually emerges as 'national hero' in *Henry V*. However, in *Henry*

IV Parts I & II Bradley points to Hal's questionable superstitious and political use of religion. Yet again Hal's early soliloquy is re-examined for its 'strain of policy' which recalls his father, a readiness to use other people for his own ends. Put more bluntly, Hal's regard for others is expedient and utilitarian. He may show some affection, but there is no love outside that of his family, though many would find even this questionable? Even when we hear of Hal's '. . . nature, love and filial tenderness' (*Henry IV Part II*, IV.5.38) it seems to come from a sense of reciprocal duty of status which is almost formally obligatory, rather than an affective impulse. Thus Bradley sees the rejection as quite consistent with this aspect of Hal's character. The problem, as he sees it, is that Shakespeare inadvertently created 'so extraordinary a being' in the Falstaff scenes that our sympathies cannot be shifted at the rejection. Our hearts remain with Falstaff. Our sympathy has ensured that we laugh with Falstaff, not at him. In sum 'the bliss of freedom gained in humour is the essence of Falstaff' (p.262). Unfortunately, this existential celebration rather jars ironically against the more hard-headed view some might take of Falstaff, for all his wit, as an opportunist old sponger. The 'atmosphere of perfect freedom' (p.263) Bradley claims we are lifted into can seem like sheer irresponsibility. The defence of Falstaff is almost entirely in naturalistic terms, of Falstaff as a real life person, albeit a person with vast reserves of self-consciously debunking humour. Thus, for Bradley, Falstaff's 'lies' on returning from the Gadshill escapade were clearly for the sake of humour, not to deceive. In defending Falstaff against the charge of cowardice Bradley invokes the arguments of Morgann that we have seen. But in a later additional footnote he has to admit that Hal's statement that Falstaff 'roared for mercy' (*Henry IV Part I*, II.4.256) cannot be disputed. The seamier side of Falstaff's character which Shakespeare increasingly stressed in *Part II* is recognised, but, following Hazlitt, Bradley insists on separating the serious from the comic:

> You no more regard Falstaff's misdeeds morally than you do the much more atrocious misdeeds of Punch or Reynard the Fox. You do not exactly ignore them, but you attend only to their comic aspect. (p.270)

At no time does Bradley recognise how the imperatives of comic role-playing might modify naturalistic explanation in terms of dramatic convention and audience engagement.

On the other hand E. E. Stoll's attack on Morgann and the whole rise of psychological, naturalistic criticism, is based on a theatre historian's reconstruction of the inheritance and influence of comic modes which he sees as not only shaping Falstaff but, in a complementary way, also predisposing audience assimilation and reaction. As critic and scholar, Stoll brings a wealth of illustration to his argument, quoting from Latin and Greek comedy of antiquity, and French, Italian and Spanish drama of the Renaissance period.

For Stoll the depiction of Falstaff derives from the conventional dramatic inheritance of the *miles gloriosus*, or braggart soldier.

He has the increasing belly and decreasing leg, the diminutive page for a foil, the weapon (his pistol) that is no weapon but a fraud, as well as most of the inner qualities of this ancient stage-figure – cowardice and unbridled bragging, gluttony and lechery, sycophancy and pride. (pp.428–9)

A few variations on the type are noted and plain differences acknowledged: Falstaff is not silly and affected, he does not boast needlessly, he is not beaten and knocked about the stage, and, last but not least, he is a humorist and wit. Alternatively, Stoll notes, most of the characteristics of the *miles* were also those of the clown. It follows that according to Elizabethan usage, foolish characters like Falstaff, Malvolio in *Twelfth Night* and Benedick in *Much Ado About Nothing*, are tricked by conspiracies, made fools of, let in on their deception and jeered at. Again, in his wider-ranging re-searches, Stoll cannot find a single instance of a character playing the coward on purpose, and then playing the ludicrous braggart afterwards. To an audience, without some indication from the dramatist, such ambiguity would have been incomprehensible be-cause whenever in Elizabethan drama a character is feigning we are informed of it. Fundamentally, Stoll denies the premise of Bradley and his predecessors that Falstaff is *playing* at being a coward, liar, thief and butt, rather than, as he insists, *being* such. Situations like the coward charging others with cowardice, as Falstaff charges Hal and Poins; of the coward taking a captive, as Falstaff does Coleville; or the rogue caught in a trap and having to explain his way out of it, like Falstaff concerning Gadshill, are all parts of the common European heritage of Renaissance theatre. Consequently, in denying Falstaff that extra dimension of self-consciousness of a character beyond that of a coward or braggart, Stoll sees the soliloquies on honour and sack as, respectively, coming not 'from his heart of hearts, but out of his wits to cover his shame', 'it is the exposure not (as has been thought) the expression, of his inmost self' (p.469).

At this point, if not earlier, certain weaknesses in Stoll's approach become apparent. For all the seeming liberal breadth of his learning, his views are narrow and doctrinaire, as well as logically susceptible. If, as he points out, Falstaff is on the battlefield and at the King's council at Shrewsbury, for the sake of his humour, why is the seeming cowardice not also for the sake of the humour? Though Falstaff's wit and humour is acknowledged, Stoll's judgement continually invokes the lowest common denominators of theatrical conventions, not, in Falstaff's case, the all-important differences from it. Development and innovation must obviously play a powerful part in the theatre otherwise it would have become moribund centuries ago. Is it not manifestly the case that Falstaff is as much a development from, as a repetition of, the dramatic archetypes Stoll examines? Where is another Falstaff to be found? A *reductio ad absurdum* lies at the heart of Stoll's position – the implication that Shakespeare's ideal audience is a group of learned American professors of theatre studies sagely marking Falstaff's pedigree, like a punter at a racecourse. By a curious irony, for all his historical study, Stoll is rather a-historical in failing to recognise the significant problems of the history of Shakespearean meaning, an issue crucial to modern commentators like Graham Holderness. More pointedly, Stoll's approach sticks to character, but although he rejects Ulrici's structural approach, he nevertheless concedes at one point that Falstaff as a clown

could be supposed to have neither philosophy nor anti-philosophy, being a comic contrast and appendage to the heroes and the heroic point of view. (p.474)

This concession is made, but not explored, in order to reinforce a larger rejection – Maginn's notion of Falstaff as a 'military free-thinker' (Fineman, p.182). In a give-away earlier passage Stoll had claimed:

For Falstaff is as simple and un-cynical as the dramatist and his times. By him the chivalric ideal is never questioned. Hotspur is

comical only for his testiness, for the extravagance of his imagination and language, not for his derring-do. To some critics Falstaff
seems a parody or burlesque of Knighthood ... but the only
parallel or contrast between knight and clown suggested is on the
battlefield: and there, as in Calderon's comedies, the ridicule is
directed at the clown alone. (p.472)

No scholar, historian or critic today would be inclined to support
the notion that Shakespeare was 'simple', let alone his epoch. In
truth it rather describes Stoll's approach. Neither would many argue
for Shakespeare as a cynic, but with the resurgence of the philo-
sophic scepticism of antiquity as an aspect of Renaissance culture,
pre-eminent in Montaigne, its profound influence on Shakespeare's
middle period has long been recognised, above all in *Hamlet* and
King Lear. Falstaff's 'honour' soliloquy, his 'catechism', as it is
usually referred to, is part of the thematic structure of the play, as
Stoll's nineteenth-century predecessors recognised. Though it is
perhaps too schematic to see Hotspur and Falstaff solely in terms of
an excess and deficiency of honour, nevertheless their several
pronouncements contribute to Shakespeare's dramatisation of the
ambivalence between words and deeds. The disparity between what
men say and what men do is arguably a fundamental principle of
drama. In *Henry IV Parts I & II* Shakespeare explores the relationship between an ideal abstract prescriptive code – chivalry – and
the reality of what men actually do, with all the mixed motives,
hypocrisy, delusion, egoism and power hunger, that flesh is heir to.
It is significant to note that the play in which Shakespeare puts this
most thoroughgoingly to the test is silently passed over by Stoll, for
all his learned references, without one mention – namely *Troilus and
Cressida*.

As Stoll perceived, 'sympathy' is the crucial term for Bradley's
(and our?) response to Falstaff. The pervasive cultural inheritance of
late-eighteenth-century sensibility and nineteenth-century sentimentalism, quite alien to Renaissance culture, still to some extent
affects our view of literary character.

In an important study Robert Langbaum shows that where
sympathy is overemphasised the focus of the plays get displaced by
making Falstaff the centre of value and meaning. Instead of our
responding to Falstaff by way of an objective set of public criteria
(honesty, valour, probity, duty etc.) we see the play-world in his

terms. To a great extent the parodic structural function of the
Falstaff scenes, which Ulrici grasped, encourages this. Unless this is
counterbalanced by a recognition of a dialectic of ideas in the plays,
the tendency is for critics to by and large narrow the plays mostly to
Part I and then to further select aspects of Falstaff's character to
arrive at such coy and misleading formulas, like that of Bradley's
'the bliss of freedom gained in humour is the essence of Falstaff'
(p.262). Bradley is not merely wayward nor eccentric, neither is he
merely a follower of Morgann and nineteenth-century psychological
naturalism. Shakespeare himself laid the ground for such an emphasis in his response to the success of Falstaff in *Part I*, by following
it up in *Part II* with one of the most popular procedures then and
now, from Tamburlaine to Rambo – give them the same again, and
more of it! However, it should be noted here that Stoll's historical
approach has remained a powerful force in twentieth-century criticism, particularly in the work of John Dover Wilson and Bernard
Spivack. Though Dover Wilson's *The Fortunes of Falstaff* (1943) is
by no means the original work he claims, as Babcock has shown, it
has been immensely influential in furthering a particular approach
to *Henry IV Parts I & II*. Like Stoll, Dover Wilson has almost an
archaeologist's approach to the notion of character and drama.
Complementing his predecessor's stress on the *miles gloriosus* Dover
Wilson sees Falstaff in terms of late-medieval morality plays. Here is
the Vice, or Riot, or Vanity, tempting the prodigal prince from Law
or Government as embodied by the Lord Chief Justice. Spivack
provides detailed evidence of Falstaff as deriving from the medieval
Psychomachia, the allegorical fight for man's soul by good and evil.
Falstaff is 'the composite image of Gluttony, Lechery, and all the
rest of the fleshly sins' (p.89). Spivak attempts to make up for Dover
Wilson's rather unsubstantiated claims by providing 'precise corres-
pondences between Falstaff and the morality vices' (p.70). It is true
that in Shakespeare's plays there are several allusions to the
moralities – perhaps most notably Hal's comment 'that reverend
vice, that grey iniquity' (*Henry IV Part I*, II.4.447). Yet Spivack's
documentation makes all the more glaring Shakespeare's great
difference from any predecessors.

It is quite fatuous to remark, as Spivack does, that 'allegory has
been overlaid by history – by historical places, literal events, and the
moral drapery of concrete humanity' (p.90). While it cannot be de-
nied that there are vestiges of older drama in *Henry IV Parts I & II*

at the same time it has to be recognised that an evolutionary jump has taken place. To turn from something like Spivack's discussion of Henry Medwall's *Nature* (1490–1501) or John Rastell's *The Four Elements* (*c.* 1517) to *Henry IV Parts I & II* is to experience difference more than likeness, the degree of naturalism in Shakespeare completely outweighing that of convention. In seeing 'concrete humanity' as merely 'moral drapery' only the most blinkered scholarship could claim otherwise. In his critique of Dover Wilson, William Empson gives voice to a marvellous phrase, 'What is really hard is to stretch one's mind all around Falstaff' (p.36). While heartily agreeing we might add that to swap 'Falstaff' for 'Shakespeare' here would be equally apt. The sense of richness, plenitude and multifariousness which characterises *Henry IV Parts I & II* and all of Shakespeare's drama derives from a profound realisation of the dimensions, manifestations and range of the human predicament, a secular realisation freed from the narrow homiletic codifications of schematic didacticism. This is not to champion a Renaissance dramatist of psychological naturalism versus a medieval conceptualism which would amount to another kind of reductive simplification that is being challenged. The question of performance makes the issue plainer. Give a director any medieval morality play or Tudor interlude, such as the above, and Shakespeare's *Henry IV Parts I & II*, and he will soon tell you the vast difference in decisions which have to be made between the relative formalised crudity of one and the ramified sophistication of the other. A newer, more complex kind of archaeological approach to Falstaff, the carnivalesque, has arisen in recent years and appears in several contemporay critics, as we shall see.

Positive political readings

Part of the late-nineteenth-century view of *Henry IV Parts I & II* focusing primarily on character saw both negative and positive aspects of such figures as Hal, Hotspur, Falstaff and the King. Whereas someone like Boas could weigh the fors and againsts, critics like Masefield, Yeats and Shaw assume that Shakespeare presents Lancastrian kingship in a harsh and critical light in the plays as a whole. In the criticism of the twentieth century we find a continuing major divide between what may be called positive and negative political readings of the plays. Positive political readings directly or indirectly see Shakespeare variously as a patriot, a defender of monarchy and all that is connoted by order, degree and hierarchy – as a conservative ideologue and apologist, in fact. Negative political readings find that Shakespeare's radical and subversive ambivalence brings into question any absolute values of such concepts as authority, honour and chivalry. Roughly speaking, positive political readings continue up to the Second World War and find a major spokesman in the celebrated study of E. M. W. Tillyard's *Shakespeare's History Plays* (1944), while negative political readings, though found before Tillyard, develop mostly in reaction to him right up to the present day.

Sir Walter Raleigh contributed a study of Shakespeare to the extremely successful 'English Men of Letters' series in 1907. After considering *Henry IV Parts I & II* he assesses the difficulty of estimating Shakespeare's political opinions and offers the seemingly tempered judgement:

> It is safe to say that Shakespeare had a very keen sense of government, its utility and necessity. If he is not a partisan of authority, he is at least a passionate friend to order ... he extols government with a fervour that suggests a real and ever-present fear of the breaking of the flood-gates. (pp.191–2)

Here 'passion' exonerates Shakespeare from authoritarianism and simultaneously implies a 'sense of government' that is the reverse of the polarised extremism of anarchy. Raleigh is further quoted by J. A. R. Marriott (1) as follows, 'in the matter of politics [Shakespeare] was on the side of the Government and of all but a very few of the people who were proud to call themselves the subjects of the Queen' (p.680). Abstract 'government' now becomes 'the government' of Elizabeth I and Shakespeare's plays are taken to support the status quo. For E. F. Tucker Brooke, Shakespeare depicts 'the ideal hypothetical type' in Hal, 'the character evolution of a great national leader' (p.332) who would embody 'the ideals of kingly service ..., justice, and patriotic fervour' (p.336). This idealised, simplified view is brought into focus all the more readily by sweeping aside the anachronistic comic scenes of Falstaff and company. In contrast J. A. R. Marriott (2) at least allows for the complexity of the historical process behind the plays. He examines the historical circumstances of Henry's ascent to the throne, Henry's conservative usurpation as he sees it: Henry as the representative of landowners threatened by the revolutionary communism of John Ball; Henry as the defender of religious orthodoxy threatened by the Lollard heresies of John Wyclif; Henry as the defender of constitutionalism threatened by the absolutism of Richard II; and Henry as the representative of a baronial oligarchy which had antagonised successive kings since the Magna Carta of 1215. All this provides a provocative context for Marriott's example of Worcester's reminding Henry of his indebtedness to baronial magnates like the Percys (*Henry IV Part I*, 1.3). However, the title of Marriott's (2) study, *English History in Shakespeare*, is rather misleading. Shakespeare becomes a gloss on English History with Marriott often confounding the two at the expense of the former. For all the political and social details of history, the premise of the study is of Shakespeare as 'a great-hearted English patriot' (p.2) whose English history plays 'fulfilled the heroic temper of Elizabethan England' (p.3). Marriott's study was published in the last year of the Great War and though he is not blind to the issue of Hal's Lancastrian policy and calculation, the spectacle of the future Henry V as yet again an ideal Christian knight embodying the spirit of chivalry and patriotism, prevents any complex criticism. 'For my own part', Marriott says, 'I am not prepared thus tamely to surrender one of the few remaining heroes of my boyhood' (p.143). Instead, as the hallmark of Shakespeare's seeming conservatism Marriott parallels Ulysses' degree speech in *Troilus and Cressida* (1.3.75–137) and John of Gaunt's 'This England' speech from Richard II (II.1.31–68) as Shakespeare's 'political apologia' (p.30).

Arguably the most influential and substantial contribution to the view of Shakespeare as Tudor apologist, providing both a source and impetus for Tillyard, was Alfred Hart's extended essay *Shakespeare and the Homilies* (1934). *Certyayne Sermons or Homilies, appoynted by the Kynges Maiestie to be declared and redde by all Personnes, Vicars, or Curates, every Sundaye in their Churches, where they have cure* appeared in 1547 followed in 1563 by *The Seconde Tome of Homilies containing XX discourses*. The tenth homily of the first collection entitled 'An exhortation concerning good order and obedience to Rulers and Magistrates' contains the kernel of Tudor church and state orthodoxy, preaching the doctrines of the divine right of kings, non resistance, passive obedience and the wickedness

of rebellion. In 1573, following the rebellion of 1569, Pope Pius V's
Bill of Deposition against Elizabeth I, and rumours of an invasion of
England, a new lengthy homily was added – 'Against Disobedience
and Wilful Rebellion'. In studying the many references in Shakespeare, particularly in the English histories, to such things as the
sanctity of kingship and the horrendousness of rebellion Hart finds
that:

> What is peculiar to Shakespeare is that he treats the politico-
> theological doctrines of divine right, non-resistance, passive
> obedience and the sin of rebellion, as the accepted and immutable
> law of almost every land in every age. (p.28)

So much so, Hart feels that the plays offer a digest of Tudor
orthodoxy. Essentially, the tenth homily above and Elizabeth's
addition, espouse the doctrine of the divine ordering of the all-
inclusive hierarchies of heaven and earth, from Archangel to villein.
Order functions by obedience to the king without which there is
chaos. Only God can punish a wicked king and rebellion is always
wrong. Hart's findings provided the bricks and the Tudor Myth
gave the mortar to Tillyard's fabric.

E. M. W. Tillyard's *Shakespeare's History Plays* (1944) has proved
to be the most formidably influential study to date, for several
reasons. First, the three Henry VI plays had been finally accepted
into the canon, thus confirming the idea of the full epic sweep of
Shakespeare's achievement in two tetralogies which invited a corres-
pondingly monumental critical response. Second, no one before
Tillyard had given the same degree of attention to the histories both
in terms of scale and depth. Third, the selection of Tillyard's study
to join the inauguration of Penguin Books' academic wing, Peregrine,
was brought about by the explosion of English studies in higher
education of the 1960s. That is to say, a generation of English
lecturers could now pass on the approach they had been taught
which would then be fed back into the educational system when, in
turn, their students became teachers of English literature. Fourth,
and most importantly, in a period of European devastation and
carnage in the Second World War, Tillyard found, in Shakespeare's
dramatisation of fifteenth-century warfare, ultimate providential
order. Tillyard offered the ideological assurance based on transcend-
ence, not the contingencies of history.

Not only was *Shakespeare's History Plays* a work of considerable scope in itself, as will be examined, but it was preceded by a separate prolegomena or introduction, *The Elizabethan World Picture* (1943). This work presents cultural commonplaces from an amalgam of classical and Christian sources leavened by the Roman Catholic civilisation of Europe in the Middle Ages. The world picture is seemingly all-inclusive from the lowest object in creation, like a stone, to the highest metaphysical abstraction like Godhead itself. All have place, nature, function and relationship within a given hierarchy which itself, according to the principle of correspondence, reflects another higher or lower hierarchy. This is the divine ordinance; everything is sanctioned by God, thus the divinity of kingship. Everything is determined by the underlying principle of order. This order is reinforced by unity and the common metaphor for unity is that of the great chain of being with its key concept of 'linking'. By this linkage and the additional concept of correspondence, or analogy, everything was bound together by degree and resemblance. Tillyard provides the best recapitulation in *Shakespeare's History Plays*

> Of all the correspondences between two planes that between the cosmic and the human was the commonest. Not only did man constitute in himself one of the planes of creation, but he was the microcosm, the sum in little of the great world itself. He was composed materially of the four elements and contained within himself, as well as his rational soul, vegetative and sensitive souls after the manners of plants and animals. The constitution of his body duplicated the constitution of the earth. His vital heat corresponded to the subterranean fire; his veins to rivers; his sighs to winds; the outbursts of his passions to storms and earthquakes. (p.16)

The Elizabeth World Picture remains a useful handbook as an introductory guide to cultural allusion but it does not quite justify its title. One chapter unmentioned so far is that entitled 'sin'. This for Tillyard is:

> the theological scheme of sin and salvation ... the orthodox scheme of the revolt of the bad angels, the creation, the temptation and the fall of man, the incarnation and the atonement, and

regeneration through Christ ... Here was another pattern as powerful in its imaginative appeal as the divine order of the universe ... it had been the pattern St. Paul imposed as the Christian material. (p.29)

This representation seems ecumenical until the reader registers not what is said, but what is missing – all historical particularity. There is no mention of the Reformation, the Counter Reformation or Humanism. Puritanism is hardly touched on. The significance of Non-Conformity from Wyclif onwards is passed over. Such occasions as Luther's debate with Erasmus receive no attention here. Although seemingly presenting certain continuities in the history of ideas Tillyard wilfully ignores social and political discontinuities. The theology he sketches in was itself the outcome of those early conciliar movements which for better or for worse helped shape Christianity, the Catholic Church, the Holy Roman Empire and all that they gave rise to: the problem of church versus state; the Reformation; the rise of the nation states. Because Tillyard is concerned with continuities his *Elizabethan World Picture* has no discussion of the development from feudalism to capitalism. His chosen historical perspective, selected Elizabethans in their own terms, precludes him from the insights we expect of an historian. Another scholar could assemble another *Elizabethan World Picture* quite different to Tillyard's which would concentrate on precisely the opposite of his enterprise: the sense of old certainties coming to an end, above all in the resurgence of the classical scepticism of Pyrrho and Sextus Empiricus which found voice in people like Montaigne and Shakespeare.

Imagine a volume which consisted not of a series of landscape paintings, but of a series of landscape montages entitled *The English Landscape*. How acceptable would this be? Alternatively, think of a similarly entitled volume of photographs. At what point would it become sufficiently inclusive to warrant the title? Tillyard's *The Elizabethan World Picture* is selected by choice according to a preconceived aim; it is an ideological representation for ideological ends which become clear with his main study.

Shakespeare's History Plays is divided into two parts. Part One provides a series of backgrounds: cosmic; historical; non-dramatic; dramatic. Part Two looks at the history plays. The 'cosmic' background goes over aspects of the *Elizabethan World Picture*, once again stressing the principle of order and degree to which Shake-speare had access in the *Sermon on Obedience* in the first book of Homilies, a source for Ulysses' degree speech in *Troilus and Cressida* (I.3.75–137), Tillyard surmises. The 'historical back-ground' would have been more accurately titled the historiographical background since Tillyard offers thumbnail sketches of medieval and Renaissance historians with two key sections interposed, on 'The Tudor Myth' and 'The Doctrine of Rebellion'. The non-dramatic literary background includes *A Mirror for Magistrates*, a popular compendium of the rise and fall of great ones (and not so great, like Jack Cade), which is devoted to instruction by example of cause and effect in history, above all stressing the necessity of obedience to the monarch. The chapter on dramatic background is largely redundant since most of the works discussed, apart from *Gorboduc, Woodstock* and *Sir Thomas More* express little if any of the doctrines of order and the Tudor Myth (a fact which should have given Tillyard more food for thought). Thus Tillyard assembles a formidable array of cultural reference to preface his discussion of the plays. What does it add up to? One crucial leading idea, in fact, that of the Tudor Myth. Tillyard abstracts the myth primarily from his reading of the Tudor historian Edward Hall. The Tudor Myth refers to the belief that the unification of the houses of York and Lancaster in the marriage of Henry Tudor and his accession to the throne as Henry VII was part of the divine workings of providence in English history. The usurpation and murder of Richard II had brought a curse upon the land and the Wars of the Roses were both punish-ment and expiation for the crime against the Lord's anointed. An important correlative to this belief was the doctrine of passive obedience as espoused in the last addition of 1574 to the Book of Homilies – 'Against Disobedience and Wilful Rebellion'. In short it stated that no form of rebellion in any circumstances against the divinely appointed monarch was acceptable, whatever the character and behaviour of the king. These conservative, orthodox views of the Tudor church and state are believed by Tillyard to be espoused by Shakespeare in the English history plays.

It has been pointed out that simply on logical grounds Tillyard's position is open to question. Raymond Powell comments that 'In the matter of what the age believed, it is inconceivable that everyone subscribed to the doctrine of Degree in a totally unquestioning spirit' (p.44), and he continues by arguing that the plays themselves are evidence against Tillyard's homogenisation of history. Before taking this empirical cue it should be added here that another commentator, in a valuable article, shows that Tillyard, to maintain his position, had to ignore leading political historians of his day. Robin Headlam Wells in 'The Fortunes of Tillyard: Twentieth-Century Critical Debate on Shakespeare's History Plays' makes the serious point that the scholarship of J. W. Allen (*A History of Political Thoughts in the Sixteenth Century*, 1928) and George Sabine (*A History of Political Theory*, 1937), show the *heterogeneity* of Tudor political thought, including discussion of the all-important issue of the right of resistance against a despotic monarch. To turn from J. W. Allen to Tillyard is to turn from the complexity and paradoxes of English political thought in a European context to simplification which can only be called wilfully blinkered.

However, Tillyard has had many followers including Ribner, Reese, Sprague, Richmond, and recently Robert Rentoul Reed. Most criticism of Tillyard is general, testing the theoretical content in an abstract fashion; for example, David L. Frey summarises the core of his critique of Tillyard's view of the first tetralogy as follows:

> if a king, God's anointed representative, a fully devout Christian, but a failure as a monarch, undergoes extreme suffering and is finally slaughtered by a villain of diabolical dimensions, *all without God's intervention*; and if a fully Machiavellian anti-Christian, but a 'success' as a monarch, inflicts extreme suffering on numerous innocents, including the former monarch, the heir to the throne and his own wife, *all without God's intervention*, then the Tudor argument that God actually intervened in the history of England, is at least, effectively shaken, for either the simple-minded Tudor view of providence is insufficient, and needs serious modification in order to explain the existence of innocent suffering, or God's failure to protect Henry VI, his saintly king, is a serious lapse in his guidance and control of the affairs of England. (p.3)

What is behind this is the commonly found humanist distaste for any notion of providence actually working *through* rather than *in spite of* evil and human suffering. The opposite to this is the theological apriorism which insists, believing in providence as an article of faith, that whatever the circumstances God works through a glass, however darkly. Elizabethans had no difficulty in accepting that God used evil people for his own ends. Thus Robert Rentoul Read defends the idea of divine retribution in Richard of Gloucester, 'ordain'd' (*Henry VI Part III*, V.6.57–58) as a scourge of God to kill Henry VI. Others might take the word 'ordain'd' as an ironic sublimation of a 'murderous Machiavel' (*Henry VI Part III*, III.2.193), a citation Tillyard ignores as it does not fit his argument – 'we do not need to give much heed to Machiavelli' (p.23). If we turn from generalised cultural criticism for and against Tillyard's position we have two fundamental sources of evidence for his argument, namely the Tudor chronicles and Shakespeare's plays.

Turning to the Tudor chronicles and their fifteenth-century predecessors H. A. Kelly has undertaken the most thoroughgoing re-examination there has been to date. Kelly's primary discovery is that there were three 'myths', not just one 'Tudor myth'. Hall and Holinshed were heirs of a Lancastrian myth, a Yorkist myth, and a Tudor myth, let alone a dualistic view of Richard II, one seeing his death as a tragedy, another seeing his death as a punishment for the murder of Woodstock. However, the Lancastrian myth saw the overthrow of the corrupt Richard by Bolingbroke as divinely ordained, a blessing continued in his reign and in that of Henry V. The Yorkists saw the Lancastrians as usurpers and providence came to their aid in reclaiming the crown. The Tudor myth attempted an ultimate reconciliation and dynastic marriage, and the accession of Henry Tudor demonstrated a providential reordering and settlement, so to speak, of the various claims of York and Lancaster. In his conclusion H. A. Kelly summarises 'it would seem that the providential aspect of the Tudor myth as described by Mr. Tillyard is an ex post facto Platonic Form, made up of many fragments that were never fitted together into a mental pattern until they felt the force of his own synthesizing energy' (p.298). Attempting to find evidence for Tillyard's argument Kelly notes:

> In Shakespeare hereditary providential punishment seems to be predicted once by Richard II, and feared by Henry V in his own person and by Henry IV and Clarence in the persons of their children. But it is never dramatized as taking effect, except perhaps in the mind of Queen Margaret ... (p.300)

What Shakespeare did, Kelly finds, was to allocate to various spokesmen their appropriate myths, 'thus the sentiments of the

Lancaster myth are spoken by Lancastrians, and opposing views are voiced by anti-Lancastrians and Yorkists. And the Tudor myth finds its fullest statement in the mouth of Henry Tudor' (p.305).

When we turn from the chronicles and Tillyard's 'use' of them to his examination of the plays in Part Two of his study it comes as something of a shock to find that there is no critical exposition of any substance concerning the detail of the works. By and large discussion of *Henry VI Parts I, II & III* is taken up with plot summaries, and examination of style with an occasional assumption about England as a morality 'Respublica'. In fifty-one pages of discussion the best that Tillyard can come up with are the two following passages concerning *Henry VI Part II* and *Henry VI Part III*.

In presupposing the background of degree and of God's order the second part is like the first, but it allows that background to be dimmer. Gloucester is more the honest statesman than the pure symbol of degree. And it is Iden, the virtuous Kentish squire, who in a far smaller way than Talbot fulfils this symbolic function. But there are enough incidental touches to remind us of the whole cosmic context, as when in the hawking scene near St. Albans Henry thus comments, as the nobles begin to bicker:
>   The winds grow high; so do your stomachs, lords.
>   How irksome is this music to my heart!
>   When such strings jar, what hope of harmony?
Here we have the duplication of uproar in macrocosm and microcosm, and the cosmos as a harmonious dance or a piece of music (p.175).

The extensive background material of Part One serves as an ideological integument through which filters something as disproportionately inconsequential as this. Again in considering bloodshed in *Henry VI Part III* we find:

There is, however, sufficient reference to the positive principles of order for us not to forget the less immediate and more beneficient workings of heaven. It is Henry VI who is the direct instrument of their expression. Whereas in the second part he was conspicuous for his weakness, he is now more conspicuous by his high principles and his humanity. At Towton ... he set up the miniature order of the shepherd's life against the major chaos of battle. In front of York he protests against the brutality of the head of his dead enemy York being set up on the walls. (p.189)

Tillyard chooses to ignore Henry's behaviour in Act one of *Henry VI Part III* where he is intimidated by Warwick and humiliated by the queen for his political quiescence. In the midst of carnage, Henry, futilely sitting on a molehill celebrating the shepherd's life, ironically re-evokes the savage death of York when he was viciously mocked by Margaret and others as he was forced to stand on a molehill – a detail not in Hall but obviously added by Shakespeare to create the cruelly sardonic parallel. Henry may well protest at the atrocity of York's head, but in the same scene his continued political ineptitude yet again contributes to his misfortunes. Although Henry celebrates Richmond, the future Henry VII, as Tillyard goes on to point out, immediately before that he makes one of his grossest errors by appointing two protectors in order to retire to 'private life' and 'devotion'. In the midst of blood, barbarism and betrayal, Henry is seized by the Yorkists, imprisoned in the Tower and is slain by Richard of Gloucester. It is hard indeed to see the 'beneficient workings of heaven' in this. Rather, Henry's unremitting piety is seen to be his gravest political weakness. Tillyard misrepresents the evidence by completely ignoring major aspects of the text which would controvert it.

Turning to the account of *Henry IV Parts I & II* we find the general critical framework of a morality pattern in which Hal is tested in the chivalric virtues in *Part I*, and in justice in *Part II* in his development as the 'Kingly type'. The Tudor myth and its corollaries hardly get a mention at all. At one point Tillyard quotes Henry's lament in *Part II*, 'O God, that one might read the book of fate' (III.1.45ff), and Warwick's reply 'There is a history in all men's lives' (III.1.50ff). This is an 'illustration' of 'the general historical doctrine ... the principle of history repeating itself' as a form of 'retribution' (pp.291–2). Yet the part of Henry's speech that is quoted is about disaster not retribution, 'new chances mock/ And changes fill the cup of alteration/with divers liquors'. This testifies to the patternless arbitrariness of disaster, not to a pattern of retributive justice. Warwick's famous answer needs quotation:

> There is a history in all men's lives
> Figuring the nature of the times deceas'd;
> The which observ'd, a man may prophesy,
> With a near aim, of the main chance of things
> As yet not come to life, who in their seeds
> And weak beginnings be intreasured.
>
> (III.i.80–85)

Warwick's reply goes on to say that Richard might have guessed that Northumberland's falseness would repeat itself with Henry. Warwick is responding to the unquoted part of Henry's speech when he recalls Richard's prophecy about Northumberland's betrayal. In short, Warwick is saying implicitly that natural disaster cannot be foretold but, explicitly, human conduct can, by the observable facts of human nature. This goes directly against Tillyard's whole thesis in implicitly denying theological explanation by insisting on what we would call psychological naturalism. Once again, when Tillyard examines the text to promote his thesis it collapses. In terms of argument and evidence, of historical scholarship, as well as on logical grounds, Tillyard's work is a fabrication. What we have here is the King's New Clothes in reverse. Tillyard's thesis, as he presents it, is all clothes and no body.

Sometimes it is very difficult to understand how such studies were so well (if not uniformly) received. Take Lily B. Campbell's *Shakespeare's Histories: Mirrors of Elizabethan Policy* (1947). Here the author, in an extensive display of historiographic learning, undertakes to examine Shakespeare as an expositor of Tudor Historians. Again, the Tudor myth rears its head and Henry IV is seen to suffer for usurpation, and rebellion gets its providential come-uppance. In Campbell usurpation is rather complicated in that to reconcile the variety of historiographic opinion a cyclical theory is devised, invoking *Romans* 12:19 concerning retribution visited upon the heads of the third generation. Shakespeare is an advocate of Tudor orthodoxy once again. But what are we to make of the view that 'a series of comic interludes interrupts the continuity of the historical pattern of the two parts of *Henry IV* . . . Falstaff is historically an intruder' (p.213). Such limitation surely casts doubt on the critical value of Campbell's research as a whole. When a major aspect of the plays is discounted what is said can only be partial and distorted, as many have acknowledged.

Why has Tillyard's study been so successful, and, indeed continues to find defenders? In a word, conservatism. Tillyard is basically conservative and as such has always drawn a number of conservative critics to his work. As Graham Holderness (1) has shown, in a time of international warfare Tillyard's covert ideology offered the certainties of ultimate order and continuity in which 'this England' was divinely ordained, surviving the horrors of civil war in the fifteenth century, the threat of the Spanish armada in the 1580s, and the Blitz of the Second World War.

Negative political readings

Even as Tillyard published his major work a junior colleague in his own Cambridge college, A. P. Rossiter, was giving what was to be a seminal lecture on *Henry IV Parts I & II*. Rossiter's criticism was anticipated by the views of L. C. Knights and Derek Traversi in what was to become the most significant of twentieth-century English journals, namely *Scrutiny* under the editorship of F. R. Leavis. The Thirties also saw the rise of Marxist criticism of the plays, a criticism which eventually finds its fullest expression as Cultural Materialism today. Complementing the nineteenth-century character approach is what might be called the 'new naturalism' of modern criticism found in such critics as Moody Prior and Robert Ornstein. Recent years have seen several publications concerned with a formalist, metadramatic approach. All can be grouped under 'negative political readings' since they find, in relative degrees, a questioning of the status quo – whether a direct critique of society, an ironic disjunction between public and private, or a tragic sense of life.

A. P. Rossiter's lecture 'Ambivalence: the Dialectic of the Histories' was published in 1954 and again in 1961 after the author's death, in a collection entitled *Angel With Horns* edited by Graham Storey. Apart from Tillyard's study, this lecture has become the most referred to piece of criticism on *Henry IV Parts I & II* since the war. For Rossiter the critical approaches of Tillyard and Dover Wilson are oversimplifications of the complexities of *Henry IV Part I & II*, complexities 'which often result from the use of comic parallelism of phrase or incident. That is, of parody, critically used; or of travesty-by-parallel' (p.46). Rossiter continues:

Parody of this kind operates by juxtapositions of opposites; by contrasts so extreme as to seem irreconcilable. In this sense Falstaff at Shrewsbury is a 'parody' of knighthood; everything a knight in battle ought *not* to be; that is, IF men are all that theoretical codes assume. (p.46)

As we have seen Hermann Ulrici anticipates this at length, yet he appears to be unknown to Rossiter and contemporaries (with the exception of C. L. Barber) even though a relevant gobbet of his criticism was included by Hemingway in his New Variorum Edition of *Henry IV Part II* (1936). Rossiter's 'ambivalence' is an aspect of dramatic irony which 'causes an exact juxtaposition of opposites in the mind of the audience' (p.51). Thus the comedy and seriousness of Falstaff enlisting recruits is a comment on warfare, for example. In sum 'the difficulty of establishing the Right in anything, in an England under no rightful king, is paralleled and parodied throughout in Falstaff's "manner of wrenching the true cause the false way"' (p.53). At the end of the lecture Rossiter gets towards a view of public life as role-playing with a concomitant moral, emotional and political hardness which Shakespeare's ambivalence highlights rather than endorses:

Because the Tudor myth system of Order, Degree etc. was too rigid, too black-and-white, too doctrinaire and narrowly moral for Shakespeare's mind: it falsified his fuller experience of men. Consequently, while employing it as a FRAME, he had to undermine it, to qualify it with equivocations: to vex its applications with sly or subtle ambiguities: to cast doubts on its ultimate human validity, even in situations where its principles seemed most completely applicable. His intuition told him it was *morally* inadequate. (p.59)

Rossiter's formulation of a memorable tag – 'travesty-by-parallel' – is commonly quoted buts it application as diagnostic parody was standard though not fully outlined or developed, except by Ulrici. Some years earlier in *Scrutiny* L. C. Knights had seen *Henry IV Parts I & II* as general satire 'directed against statecraft and warfare' (p.363) throughout in the use of subplot. For example:

The conspiracy of the Percies is sandwiched between the preparation of the Gadshill plot and counter-plot and its execution. Poins has 'lost much honour' that he did not see the 'action' of the Prince with the drawers'. (p.364)

Though, for Knights, the Falstaff 'attitude' permeates the plays as a whole, even when he is not on stage, nevertheless the sufficiently exaggerated language of Hotspur is parodic in itself. Otherwise in all but name Knights puts his finger on the Falstaffian travesty-by-parallel, 'The satire in the description of his ragged regiment is pointed by a special emphasis on military terms – "soldiers", "captain", "lieutenant", "ancients, corporals ... gentlemen of companies"' (pp.364–5).

Two post-war articles in *Scrutiny* by D. A. Traversi on *Henry IV Parts I & II* were later developed and included in a book length study of the Lancastrian tetralogy. Though *Shakespeare from Richard II to Henry V* remains one of the most comprehensively thorough, sensitive and perceptive studies to have appeared, Traversi's articles are more concentrated and forceful. At the outset his ideological base seems close to Tillyard in that he acknowledges the divinely appointed king ruling over a society structured by degree, against which 'the murder of Richard II [was] ... a crime against the divine foundation of order centred on the crown', and rebellion is seen as 'the supreme crime' (p.51). But then instead of following this through with anything approaching the Tudor Myth, in the articles he suggests a fundamental disjunction between private and public morality, implying that the expediency, opportunism and necessity of the latter gives rise to coldness, calculation and inhumanity. That is to say, political success necessarily entails moral shortcomings. Without falling for complete polarisation, which would be too schematic, Falstaff and Hal are seen in these terms. However, in expanding the original articles Traversi slightly shifted his ground and moved from a position by which the Battle of Shrewsbury exemplified human 'futility' and the whole of *Part II* bore witness to Shakespeare's developing tragic sense of life. In the article on *Henry IV Part I* Falstaff's 'super abundant comic vitality', 'real human understanding' (p.32) and 'humanity' function to highlight both Hal's 'detached humanity' (p.33) and, by parody, the political action of the main plot. Drawing attention in *Part II* to Shakespeare's repeated imagery of illness, disease, decay and death in the human body and the body politic, the prevailing tone is found to be not grotesque or farcical, but that of tragic pathos in human incapacity and failure. If Traversi found 'futility' as the real meaning of Shrewsbury, then *Part II* testifies to a spiritual futility succeeding upon moral emptiness.

However, Traversi's full-length study mitigates this austere position by acceding to some established approaches to Falstaff and Hal. Traversi acknowledges the medieval dramatic background of Falstaff's provenance in such figures as Vice and Riot, while he grafts onto his view of Hal the notion of the education of a prince. These points of view appear at the opening and close of the discussion functioning as a frame. More extensively here Falstaff manifests the 'vital paradox' of both representing corruption in the body politic and yet offering 'an essential criticism' (p.64). Far from being bound by morality origins, in reliving the Gadshill episode, for example, Falstaff 'becomes . . . an imaginative manifestation of the free spirit of comedy', he 'represents life, the refusal to be bound by moral categories' (p.70). On the other hand Hal is preparing to become 'the supreme embodiment of political virtue', 'the incarnation of political competence' (pp.52, 49). This seems a positive rather than negative political reading, yet within the framework of these conventional positions Traversi offers a negative perspective on political morality. Hal's 'reformation' as reflected in his soliloquy derives, in Shakespeare's more complex treatment of the 'naively optimistic' popular material, from 'political calculation' (p.58) for functional public ends, as 'an instrument of policy' (p.58) – a disjunction between the human and the political, the private and the public, carrying the paradoxical, if not tragic suggestion that political success not only entails human failure but encroaches upon it. In short, power dehumanises both great and small, guilty and innocent. Thus the condition of the rejected and the rejector. The rehearsal of the rejection in *Part I*, Traversi claims, makes us realise 'the circumstances which demand Falstaff's banishment also involve a turning aside from life, a loss which no necessity, political or even moral can make altogether irrelevant' (p.74). But given the two sides of Falstaff, comic embodiment of a vital principle and yet, as emerges unavoidably in *Henry IV Part II*, a source of corruption, when the actual rejection takes place:

the icy wind of righteous authority that will blow at Westminster . . . inhuman as the wind may seem and to some extent be, the corruption it blows away will, at least in the political order, justify it. (p.161)

The new king rejects Riot. In this way Traversi modifies his earlier more austere tragic view by shifting the critical fulcrum, from a comedic to a more simply moral view of Falstaff. The more deeply felt sense of dramatic ambivalence in Traversi's response to the rehearsed rejection of *Henry IV* is mitigated by the more conventionally didactic account of the rejection itself.

A group of critics who examine the plays in larger social terms, rather than that of the individual and political morality, are the Marxists. A. A. Smirnov presents a Shakespeare as humanist ideologist of the bourgeoisie. As such his class supported a strong centralising absolutist power against the anarchic feudal nobility. The history plays provide an analysis of monarchy and feudalism. In *Henry IV Parts I & II* Smirnov identifies the paradox of feudalism in that the Percys, Mortimers and Glendowers are 'doomed by the very attributes they are fighting to preserve' (p.45), the independence and pride made manifest as disunity and arrogance. The curse on the Lancastrians is not so much divine judgement as the precedence of usurpation and kingmaking. What power brokers have done once they can do again. In this perspective Falstaff is not just a parody of the degenerate feudal nobility, but a declassé opportunist whose critical cynicism becomes a moral attribute when turned against his class of origin. Not allowing for this ameliorative point, another critic finds in Falstaff and his cohorts 'the feudal order, more than moribund – decadent to putrescence' (T. A. Jackson, p.170). Alternatively, though a knight, Falstaff can be taken as aligning himself not with some kind of parody of feudal retainers, but with the 'vital commoners' of *Henry IV Part II*, IV.3. In this view Hal 'embodies the potential new national state' (William B. Stone, p.893). Here the education of a prince motif takes a new twist – Hal is the educated representative of a new order replacing that of feudalism. Out of this comes a Hegelian dialectical tableau

The Prince stands, triumphant, over the bodies of both Percy and Falstaff. Nobility and commons, thesis and antithesis, mutually exhausted, lie "in blood" together, while the synthesis, the new nationalism, pays homage to both and then carries on. (p.899)

The critics tend to see Shakespeare as a Marxist visionary.

Shakespeare could see much more clearly that not only the Tudor monarchs, suppressing all centrifugal baronial tendencies in their bid for absolute rule, but the entire historical process, heading towards a new social order, was laying a heavy hand on feudal honours (Stříbrný, p.61).

Such readings promote Shakespeare as a critic of feudalism indirectly championing absolutism as a stage in the eventual bourgeois revolution of the seventeenth century, thereby combining a negative political reading and a positive one but on terms quite different to that of the Tillyardians. Lukács offers a necessary caution for such facile optimism.

Shakespeare . . . sees the triumphant humanist character of the rising new world, but also sees it causing the breakdown of a patriarchal society humanly and morally better in many respects and more closely bound to the interests of the people. Shakespeare sees the triumph of humanism, but also foresees the rule of money in the advancing new world, the oppression and exploitation of the masses, a world of rampant egoism and ruthless greed. (p.401)

A reading which falls heavily on the side of pessimism is that of John F. Danby in *Shakespeare's Doctrine of Nature* (1948). Essentially, for Danby, *Henry IV Parts I & II* are an allegory in which Authority or Power (Hal and the Lord Chief Justice) exist in a symbiotically amoral relationship with Appetite (Falstaff). These approximate to Tillyard's Order and Disorder/Riot, but they are not mutually exclusive absolutes, rather they exist on the same plane, collaborating in the iniquity of the corrupt Elizabethan world buttressed by the non-theology of Tudor officialese which functions to maintain possession. The view of history propounded in *Henry IV Parts I & II* is that 'whatever is, is right, provided it is strong' (p.88). Hal is a façade, a 'machiavel of goodness' (p.189), while Falstaff 'is the most pitiless creature in the play' (p.84). Danby's book traces a line of development in Shakespeare's career up to *King Lear*. Absent in *Henry IV Parts I & II* is the significance of pity, love and fear that is found in plays like *King John* and *Richard III*. These absolute moral values are the manifestation of God's ordinance linking the divine with history. It can be fruitful to understand a Shakespeare play retrospectively by re-examining it in the light of a subsequent work. Una Ellis Fermor, for example, provides a brilliant aperçu in an essay surveying the movement from Shakespeare's Elizabethan to Jacobean period in which the varying claims of office and the individual spirit turn from the textbook emptiness of a figure like Henry V to the wrought complexities of a Hamlet or an Antony. However, the problem with Danby's Christian Marxist view of *Henry IV Parts I & II* is that it is largely unrecognisable. It is as if a few justified observations on the more sombre parts of *Henry IV Part II* have been allowed to colour his views of the plays as a whole. And it will be argued in the Appraisal below that *Henry IV Parts I & II* are not without 'love', but it is comedic and allusive rather than overt and plangent.

In more recent years two Marxist schools of criticism have made a strong impact on teaching and research, namely, Cultural Materialism in Great Britain, and New Historicism in the USA. The foreword of *Political Shakespeare* (1985) edited by Jonathan Dollimore and Alan Sinfield, provides a manifesto for Cultural Materialism. The conservatism of much criticism is challenged by Cultural Materialism by locating the literary text in its historical context, subjecting it to the theoretical analysis of Marxism reinforced by post-Structuralism. Materialism opposes idealist, a-historical, transcendant notions of meaning by studying the contexts of a play's production within a given economic and political system, taking into account such influences as the court, patronage, the theatre, education, and the church. Furthermore, cultural materialism recognises that meaning in historical terms is never static, an immanent given, but is produced and reproduced depending on the shifting cultural field, as has been touched upon above concerning Tillyard's study as a cultural production of specific historical circumstances. New Historicism has much in common with Cultural Materialism and particularly stresses the way that authority promotes subversion as a form of legitimation, a powerful idea which was anticipated by Danby. Stephen Greenblatt, a leading figure amongst the new historicists, in a much reprinted article, 'Invisible Bullets', contends that the ideal image of the king 'involves as its positive condition the constant production of its own radical subversion and the powerful containment of that subversion' (p.41). Consequently, at the close of *Henry IV Part II*

actions that should have the effect of radically undermining authority turn out to be the props of that authority. In this play, even more cruelly than in *1 Henry IV*, moral values – justice, order, civility – are secured through the apparent generation of their subversive contraries. Out of the squalid betrayals that preserve the state emerges the "formal majesty" into which Hal at the close, through a final definitive betrayal – the rejection of Falstaff – merges himself. (p.53)

Amongst the cultural materialists Graham Holderness has contributed several studies to Shakespeare's history plays. In *Shakespeare's History* (1985) it is claimed that the plays are more than drama, 'they are, in themselves and not derivatively, historiography' (p.31). Familiar approaches must be re-examined:

> that they embody a transition from a medieval period understood to be stable, providentially protected and decorously chivalric to a world of crude *Realpolitik* ... that they construct from the raw materials of the past images of the contemporary, so that in them events and problems of the fifteenth century are addressed via the beliefs of the sixteenth. (*Shakespeare: The Play of History*, p.19)

Shakespeare's historical sense thus indirectly challenges humanist or neoclassical assumptions about the universality of human nature, by recognising the historical dynamics of change and discontinuity. For Holderness, Shakespeare had a conscious understanding of the nature of feudalism which anticipated the discoveries of seventeenth-century historians like Sir Henry Spelman. The issue of Shakespeare's additions to the source material is not directly addressed; presumably they are part of 'the historiographical effort to reconstruct the past' (p.31)? Shakespeare's history plays, the chronicles of feudalism, identify the fundamental contradiction, which predates Henry IV's accession, in the struggle between monarchical and aristocratic power. That is, the Lancastrian tetralogy is concerned not so much with the consequences of the deposition of Richard II (or the murder of Woodstock) as with the social conflicts between shifting power groups reshaping society. 'The feudal victory of Bolingbroke centralises and deepens the unstable and contradictory forces' of society (p.78). If some of this sounds familiar, once again Ulrici's lone voice in the nineteenth century anticipated much of the cultural materialist enterprise as it is found here in Holderness's work.

As an example of the materialist approach the early confrontation between the king and Hotspur in Act I of *Henry IV Part I* is considered not in terms of character (Hotspur's fiery temper etc.) or the principle of Order (Hotspur as embodying anarchy), but as 'the contradiction between royal authority and feudal power' (p.70). According to the feudal law of arms Hotspur was entitled to keep the prisoners for ransom except for the earl of Fife whom he is prepared to surrender, but Henry demands all the prisoners. For the materialists what is of greater significance here is the way that the incident derives from a social structure fractured by contradiction. 'Honour' lies in both serving and rebelling against the liege lord.

In great contrast to Holderness's study, with its constant risk of theoretical inflation, is a work referred to above, which has been well received amongst Shakespeare scholars, Robert Ornstein's *A Kingdom For a Stage* (1972). Ironically, its very virtues ultimately amount to a kind of limitation. Writing as a liberal humanist engaging primarily with the portrayal of character, Ornstein is limited by his naturalism, especially when it comes to Falstaff.

Ornstein distrusts the reductive didactic limitation of historical scholarship and insists on the primacy of Shakespeare as artist, the artist as historian. By this, given his examination of the history plays, he means the artist as a creator of historical characters. For Ornstein

> [Shakespeare's] interest in human behaviour and in political and moral issues cuts across the boundaries of dramatic genre. He places as great a value on the sanctity of personal relations in the History Plays as in the tragedies, because he intuits that order depends, not on concepts of hierarchy and degree, but on the fabric of personal and social relationships which is woven by the ties of marriage, kinship, and friendship, by communal interests, and ideas of loyalty and trust. (p.222)

This is well said although it contains a contradiction – 'social relationships' etc. are obviously influenced by 'hierarchy and degree' in a highly structured feudal society. But this is overlooked since Ornstein's theoretical position combining twentieth-century humanism with Aristotelian universalism is essentially a-historical. Yet elsewhere he is perfectly aware of the role of feudalism. A challenging point is made concerning the civil war:

Shakespeare does not suggest that men chose sides in the War of
the Roses according to their beliefs in de facto authority or
legitimacy. They took sides because of their feudal attachments,
because of the appeal of family honour and pride, or as they were
prompted by ambition, greed, patriotism, or revenge. (p.26)

The universalism that Dr Johnson would have agreed with, is
fundamental. It is glimpsed in a later remark where 'Shakespeare
speaks not about a particular historical situation, *but about unchang-
ing human realities*' (my italics, p.156).

Where Danby had scrutinised the plays in the theological terms of
'pity, love and fear', Ornstein's humanism takes the secularised
perspective of charity, love and friendship, focusing on the way
Shakespeare foregrounds intimacy, privacy and relationships. More
than in any other critic, Worcester – 'wholly rational and calculat-
ing' (p.128) – emerges as the real villain of the plays, and Falstaff is
his comic counterpart. Though Ornstein's view of character seems
standard – Henry's 'calculated lessons in statecraft' (p.129), Hal's
'coldness and calculation' (p.135) – it is difficult to do justice to
his finer discriminations without extensive quotation. Whereas
nineteenth-century criticism tended to separate character in terms of
a portrait gallery, as we have seen, Ornstein's strength is repeatedly
to see character within a structure of relationship, as part of
Shakespeare's 'ironic scrutiny'. Let one example suffice.

[Worcester] with his brother Northumberland . . . coolly observes
Hotspur's outrage in 1.3 even as he plans to exploit it. It is a
poignant irony that Hotspur should lecture his politic relatives on
the meaning of familial honour. It is more ironic still that he
cannot see in his uncle and father the duplicity he despises in the
King. Ready to hurl his defiance openly against Henry, he is led
into a secret plot that Worcester has already set down. Demand-
ing truth from Henry and then again from Glendower, he finds
only falsehood and treachery in his own kin. (pp.134–5)

Ornstein is not shy of the seemingly old-fashioned thematic
approach and turns it to good account in his appraisal of the
'question of truth' (p.131). Did Henry misrepresent his motives for
returning England to the Percys? Is he a true king? Is Hal a true
Prince? Can thieves or politicians be true to one another? Yet he

resists any larger thematic interpretation of *Henry IV Part II*.
Though acknowledging the 'pervasive thematic emphasis on weari-
ness, age and illness', this 'seems not so much an expression of the
unsettled political situation of England as an expression of the
malaise of the characters' lives' (p.156). 'Character' wins out once
again. And this is how Ornstein understands the rejection. Falstaff
in *Part II* as is always recognised, is ageing, sick, exploitative,
egoistic and corrupt, while Hal remains what he has been throughout the plays. Shrewd, pragmatic, and manipulative, not giving voice
to any choric convention, at the outset in Hal's soliloquy we find:

> the chilling effect of Hal's contemptuous lines about his comrades
> . . . Hal's diction and metaphors associate his calculated redemp-
> tion with the crassness of commodity and sharp business practices.
> (p.137)

In the rejection of Falstaff there is the 'distaste of the righteous for
the fallen' (p.169) without any Christian charity or human sympathy. In a summary reminiscent of Una Ellis Fermor, Ornstein
finds that

> [Hal] does not become cold and self-important as he begins to
> wield power; rather he is attracted to power and finds fulfillment
> in its exercise because he is from the beginning incapable of fellow
> feeling, of intimacy, of spontaneity. (p.170)

Ornstein is much more penetrating and balanced in his judgement
of Hal than is intimated by these conclusions, but in his treatment of
Falstaff we find a kind of muted resistance in the penalty exacted by
naturalism. Falstaff is a character, certainly, but he is also much
more than that. While we would not want to relegate him to the
'walking symbol' of L. C. Knights' limiting view, he is a performance, a comic projection, a richly compounded cultural figure of art,
history and anthropology – both 'plump Jack' and a mythopoeic
nexus. This is brought out by comparing Holderness's (2) approach
which is based on that of Mikhail Bakhtin, a figure who has loomed
large in cultural discourse of the last decade or so.

Bakhtin's study *Rabelais and His World*, though written in 1940,
was first published in the USSR in 1965 and was eventually
translated into English and published in 1968. Here is propounded a

theory of 'carnivalisation' in medieval and Renaissance literature. Like the Roman saturnalia, medieval folk carnival inverts authority and travesties institutions. Ecclesiastical forms are turned upside down. Authority contains oppositional ideology by licensing it in the form of carnival grotesquerie. For Bakhtin the central image of the carnival was the collective body predating the development of the atomised, individual bourgeois ego. It has long been recognised, particularly by C. L. Barber, that Falstaff has an affinity with the Lord of Misrule figure in medieval festivals. With this further cultural overlay the significance of Falstaff is given greater meaning and depth. For Holderness, Falstaff is the centre of a carnivalesque oppositional energy to the king and the feudal lords. In parody and satire Falstaff's indulgent revelry inverts the austere public world. Again, Falstaff is the collective body writ large, a figure of carnival versus the Lenten sparsity of Hal, as Rhodes and Bristol have argued.

Another naturalist, of considerable weight, is Moody E. Prior in a work which appeared one year after Ornstein's, *The Drama of Power* (1972). Taking Westmoreland's reply to Henry's recollection of Richard's prophecy (*Henry IV Part II*, III.1.80–92) – 'There is a history in all men's lives/Figuring the nature of the times diseased' – Prior finds 'explicit expression of a naturalistic scheme of causation, based on universal properties of men and the nature of political power' (p.62), rather than any pattern of providential retribution. Even the much discussed disease imagery of *Henry IV Part II* 'portraying the political disturbances of the times as disease and the rebellions as cures and purges' are taken to 'imply a naturalistic view of the nations woes' (p.64). Prior sees the world of *Henry IV Parts I & II* as a world of politics, so much so that war is 'an instrument of policy' and battles are not 'instruments of God's punitive justice' (p.70). Clearly Prior is an anti-Tillyardian, but the extraordinary aspect of his approach is that he completely straddles the positive/negative divide of political readings since the main thrust of his argument is to defend King Henry from his detractors both on and off stage. By and large critics of *Henry IV Parts I & II* take Hal and Falstaff as the principal critical concern, as we have seen, eventually coming down on one side or the other, if not attempting some sort of balance, depending on their view of the rejection. Prior is fascinating and highly original in keeping to the political predicament of the king himself in order to establish if not sympathy at least a greater understanding. Unfortunately, a final growing list of concessions tends to undermine the position he starts with.

Essentially, for Prior, in *Henry IV Parts I & II* 'Henry IV is fighting to preserve national unity and to pass on undisputed title to his son, who in turn is measuring himself for the kingly role he is destined to play' (p.211). In this contingent political world of expedience and necessity machiavellian *ragione del stato* determines means and ends, not humanist textbooks of rulership. Hotspur's partial view of that 'vile politician' Bolingbroke has been too readily shared by twentieth-century critics disillusioned by the bloody legacy of *realpolitik* and blind to the significance of Shakespeare's understanding of political ineptitude in such a king as Henry VI.

This approach certainly alerts us to the exigencies of the given political moment like that of the engineered clash between Worcester, the Percys and the king at the outset. Calculation, subterfuge and aggression must be acted against, like against like, or go under. To find support for Henry, Prior draws forceful evidence from the chronicles on the great fear of Richard II's growing arbitrariness and the increasing support for Bolingbroke to return. However, Prior's rationalisation of Henry's oath-breaking concerning the purpose of his return reads like a reincarnation of Machiavelli as literary critic:

> Bolingbroke's oath was made to be violated or at best evaded, and so the taking of it as a temporary political expedient contradicted the solemn moral obligation which the oath implied. A necessary expedient perhaps, but Bolingbroke in adopting it breaks with the past and abandons the morally unambiguous position of his initial role as unsullied public challenger of wrongs and misdemeanours in high places, which had earned him the right to be called on by his peers to restore good rule. (p.236)

A virtue of necessity indeed! However the execution of Bushy and Green is not exonerated and the betrayal of Gaultree is irreconcilable. Further, the recommendation 'to busy giddy minds/With foreign quarrels' (*Henry IV Part II*, IV.5.202–15) is a coldly calculated piece of political prudence and expediency. The moral and religious idea of a crusade is used politically. Inevitably Prior has to recognise the inescapable conflict 'between the moral man with good aims and the politician who must use evil means' (p.245). Ever sympathetic, Prior cannot bring himself to acknowledge that Henry's concern with the national interest is just the honorific side of a coin inscribed 'dynastic ambition'. As a kind of critical compensation he softens this negative political reading with 'tragic overtones' (p.248) and reverts to the positive political reading of the role of Hal in the education of a prince. Ironically, bringing the two positions together results in a bizarre understanding of Hal's first soliloquy – that the calculation he shows, far from being a limitation of his character, manifests how suited he already is for the eventual role of king. After this it comes as no surprise that Prior finds that the rejection was meant to be 'unpleasant' (p.261) as a necessity of 'the chill fearsomeness of his high office' (p.262). The implication of the whole argument is that we should accept this even if we are unable to admire it. As a corrective to the surreptitious black and white sentimentalism of criticism outraged by Henry's conduct, Prior's view is almost salutary were it not for the fact that to sustain it, apart from a few paragraphs, Falstaff is virtually ignored throughout.

Part Two: Appraisal

Honour, debt, the rejection and St Paul

The mainstream criticism of *Henry IV Parts I & II* has been one of taking sides – ultimately for or against Hal or Falstaff. Or to put it in a more familiar way, whose side do we take at the rejection? Shakespeare compounds the problem, as we shall see, by his presentation of character in the plays which is largely determined by a dualism, both onstage and in the audience. Practically every major character can be seen from opposite points of view, and indeed this dualism can be found in the way some scenes are structured. Again, the question of the structure of the two parts and their manifest differences of tone, as argued by Jenkins (*Henry IV Part II* an 'unpremeditated addition') and challenged by Hawkins (*Henry IV Parts I & II* planned from the outset), have made criticism problematic. However, in spite of some probable expediency in capitalising on the success of *Henry IV Part I*, there is a perceptible coherent development between the two plays. Not just that of the 'education of a prince', but something much more profound, anticipating Shakespeare's tragic phase. Central and most obvious is the question of 'honour', which is closely linked to literal and metaphorical notions of 'debt'. Further, the duality of Falstaff has to be reconciled by recognising how he is both a character and yet something larger, in addition, without becoming the 'walking symbol' of L. C. Knights' view. Many critics have rightly stressed the significance of time in *Henry IV Part II*, particularly in terms of age and sickness, yet, again it is hinted that this is to be reflected against something much larger, the temporal against the universal. As art intervening in history, comedy subverting chronicle, Falstaff ultimately both suggests and burlesques an ideal order of value which appraises the dramatised historical actuality of the feudal world.

Though reality falls short of the ideal and calls it into question, we are left to measure the relative claims of both in terms of the human, fallible, and attainable. Shakespeare does not make homiletic recommendations. He does not moralise or suggest a simple black and white, either/or answer to the complexity of human experience. He leaves the audience with a question salvaged from barbarism and carnage, laughter and gaiety, power and weakness – what is it that we owe to one another?

At the moment of rejection Falstaff acknowledges a debt, 'Master Shallow, I owe you a thousand pound' (*Henry IV Part II*, V.5.73). This has proved resonantly baffling for editors, though it is crucial for an understanding of the two plays. At a simple dramatic level it partly checks our hostile feelings towards Hal with an element of comedy. A fat chance Shallow has of seeing any cash from Falstaff, and yet that posture of probity in such unpropitious circumstances! The full implications of Falstaff's particular debt will be returned to after examining the larger cultural and dramatic contexts.

What do we 'owe' each other? As subjects, citizens, parents, children, friends, within a class or profession etc., kinds of obligation underpinning relationships will depend on the given cultural moment within a society subject to historical process. In the Christian, militarist, later Middle Ages of feudal England, as depicted in the chronicles, the chivalric code of honour supposedly provided the bonds of fealty. At least this was the ideal conception of something like Ramon Lull's *The Book of the Ordre of Chyvalry of Knyghthode* published by Caxton in 1484. Feudalism regulated private and public allegiances whereby an individual's relationship was determined by loyalty sustained by legitimacy. Relationship to kith, kin and king observed the feudal hierarchy, at the apex of which was the monarch. Ties or bonds were comparatively legal and institutional, rather than affective. 'England' was a composition of feudal tenures rather than a nation state. John of Gaunt's 'This England' speech in *Richard II* is more monarchist than nationalist. But once the legitimate king was removed, his replacement was just another feudal lord put there by his peers. Legitimation by *de facto* possession with the resultant transference of allegiance produces something like the farce of the Duke of York's loyalty and betrayal of his son Aumerle, with the new king's somewhat bemused forgiveness in Act V scene 3 of *Richard II*.

Debt, obligation and relationship extend beyond the social, from the personal to the sacred. Under the code of chivalry, fame and reputation, both contemporary and posthumous, were imperatives of knighthood put to proof. On the other hand there was a debt and obligation to the estate of one's soul, considered in Christian terms. These came together in the injunction to the knight to take part in a holy crusade, thereby earning absolution, with which *Henry IV Parts I & II* begins.

Richard II ends with King Henry announcing an intention to 'make a voyage to the Holy Land' (V.6.49). At the opening of *Henry IV Part I*, a crusade 'As far as to the sepulchre of Christ' (I.1.19) is invoked 'To chase these pagans in those holy fields' (I.1.24) – that is, a formal crusade to rescue the holy places from the Turks rather than merely personal expiation for Richard's death. Henry goes on to remind his audience of 'the bitter cross' when Christ the Redeemer repaid a debt as ransom for the sins of mankind. At the close of *Henry IV Part II*, Henry at the point of death brings up the crusade, but this time as a political manoeuvre.

> To lead out many to the Holy Land,
> Lest rest and lying still might make them look
> Too near unto my state
>
> (IV.5.210–12)

Here Henry's motives are as far removed from authentic piety as the Jerusalem chamber in which he dies is from Jerusalem itself. Thus, in terms of the plays as a whole, Shakespeare provides an ironic frame of Christian reference for the ideas of debt and redemption, as well as obligation, in the crusade. Within the plays we are reminded twice of the proverbial wisdom which complements Christian faith, the knowledge that life is owed to God and is a debt that is repaid by death. Falstaff is told by Hal '. . . thou owst God a death' (*Henry IV Part I*, V.1.126), and the nonchalant Feeble at his recruitment avows '. . . we owe God a death' (*Henry IV Part II*, III.2.230). In the following discussion space does not permit an extensively close analysis of every occurrence, therefore selected examples will be used to further the argument.

Elsewhere in the plays, except for one crucial instance, the language of debt ('redeem', 'due', 'reckoning' 'owe', etc.) has material connotations, both literal and metaphorical, far removed from sacred meaning, which converts abstract conceptions like honour, duty and loyalty into the quantifiable and commercial. Principle becomes a negotiable possession, like a property. The crown and the country are there to be seized and carved up. The language of debt emerges from the clash of dynastic rivalry at the outset. Worcester's first words are 'Our house' (*Henry IV Part I*, 1.3.10) which he insolently utters before 'my sovereign leige' as he goes on to remind the king of who put him on the throne. Thereafter Shakespeare repeatedly uses the names of family relationships to stress the breakdown of feudal obligation in the business of power politics: not reciprocal service and loyalty in exchange for tenure, but power for power, favour for favour. This contradiction of feudalism turned against itself is brought out very forcefully in Lord Mortimer's urging Glendower to gather 'Your tenants, friends, and neighbouring gentlemen' (*Henry IV Part I*, III.1.86) – *against* the feudal lord, not for him. Before Shrewsbury yet again Worcester reminds the king '. . . all our house, . . . myself, my brother, and his son,/. . . brought you home' (*Henry IV Part I*, V.1.31–40). Henry will not 'ranson' or 'redeem' (*Henry IV Part I*, 1.3.78, 85) the captured Mortimer who he knows has a legitimate claim to the throne. Hotspur warns his father, Northumberland, and his uncle, Worcester, that the king intends to repay the 'debt' he owes them 'Even with the bloody payment of your deaths' (*Henry IV Part I*, I.3.183, cf.IV.3.52ff). Worcester repeats the advice later in the scene 'The king will always think him in our debt . . . Till he hath found a time to pay us home' (ll. 280, 282).

This material and reductive mode of transaction is continually contrasted with the idea of honour. Hotspur tells Worcester and Northumberland 'time serves wherein you may redeem/your banish'd honours' (*Henry IV Part I*, I.3.179–80). 'Redeem' is a highly provocative word in the plays, having various shades of meaning from the sacred to the harshly profane. Hotspur's romantic egoism carries him away, and he would 'pluck bright honour from the pale-fac'd moon . . . So that he that doth redeem her thence might wear/Without corrival all her dignities' (*Henry IV Part I*, I.3.200, 204–5). His exclusiveness reverses chivalric priorities and honour is at the service of an individual, not an individual serving honour. Hal also is concerned with a form of redemption.

In the soliloquy which has caused so much comment Hal sees his low-life associations and subsequent 'reformation' as a preconceived social and political strategy, payment of a 'debt' he 'never promised', thereby 'redeeming time' seemingly wasted (*Henry IV Part I*, I.2. 204, 212). As Jorgensen (2) has shown, Hal misrepresents the Pauline injunction of *Ephesians* (v.16). Past time cannot be redeemed, but in the immediate present one's life may be amended. At times accountancy seems closer to Hal's heart than morality. When the king confronts him with the heroic image of Hotspur, Hal replies:

> I will redeem all this on Percy's head . . .
> For every honour sitting on his helm . . .
> Percy is but my factor, good my lord,
> To engross up glorious deeds on my behalf,
> And I will call him to so strict account
> That he shall render every glory up,
> Yea, even the slightest worship of his time,
> Or I will tear the reckoning from his heart.
>   (*Henry IV Part I*, III.2.132–52)

While Hotspur and the rebels are corporate raiders on the body politic, the commercial metaphors here suggest ambivalently that Hal is a prospective asset-stripper. And even the greatest symbolic asset of all, the crown itself, is weighed and measured in the scales of transaction.

>   Thy due from me
> Is tears and heavy sorrows of the blood,
> Which nature, love, and filial tenderness
> Shall, O dear father, pay thee plenteously.
> My due from thee is this imperial crown
>   (*Henry IV Part II*, IV.5.36–40)

In both cases, with Hotspur's reputation and the crown, the language is reductive, to a certain degree. However formalised and solemn the language leading up to the second quotation, and however ritualised the personal emotion of Hal, nevertheless irony is inescapable. The warmth of tears is chilled by the coldness of metal. The plentifulness of weeping comes not from depth of emotion but as the due price for gold. Two separate things, grief and succession, private feeling and public office, are levelled by the priorities of the latter in the public world of 'payment', the world represented by John of Lancaster at Gaultree Forest.

As editors point out, in the chronicles it is Westmoreland who treaties with the rebels at Gaultree. Shakespeare made the youthful Prince John the chief negotiator, thus allying his coldly calculated betrayal of honour with the house of Lancaster he represents. In agreeing to redress the grievances of the rebels Prince John swears 'by the honour of my blood' (*Henry IV Part II*, IV.2.55). By means of a sophistry – John separates the grievances from those who made them – the rebels are arrested and executed, and the disbanded army is pursued. On his arrest Mowbray protests 'Is this proceeding just and honourable?', and the Archbishop of York seconds him with 'Will you thus break your faith?'. Prince John's immediate answer is terse indeed: 'I pawn'd thee none' (*Henry IV Part II*, IV.2.110–13). For John words are objects whose value is not intrinsic but expedient. 'Faith' and 'honour' are not ideals or concepts but counters in the game of political pawnbroking which the rebels unwittingly lose. John pledged the truce with a drink as a ritualised visual symbol, for the onlooking soldiers, of 'our restored love and amity' (*Henry IV Part II*, IV.2.65). No sophistry can get round that. And when he declares '. . . by mine honour/I will perform with a most Christian care' 'redress of these grievances' (*Henry IV Part II*, IV.2.113–15) the religious enlistment and rationalisation are chilling. As we have seen, Shakespeare makes an indirect dramatic comment on this in the following scene when Sir John Coleville surrenders passively to Falstaff, the reputed victor over Hotspur. Prince John's honour is as empty as Falstaff's valour.

Falstaff on rejection acknowledges a debt, but this is one of many. In fact at one point he claims that Hal owed him a thousand pounds (*Henry IV Part I*, III.3.132). However he, in turn, is dunned by no less than the Lord Chief Justice on Mistress Quickly's behalf, 'Pay her the debt you owe her' (*Henry IV Part II*, II.1.117). Yet Falstaff, genially parasitic, engagingly exploitative, goes on to borrow more from Mistress Quickly. Falstaff's celebrated 'catechism' begins with an avowal to delay another debt, death owed to God. The 'honour' speech follows:

> . . . honour pricks me on. Yea, but how if honour pricks me off when I come on, how then? Can honour set to a leg? No. Or an arm? No. Or take away the grief of a wound? No. Honour hath no skill in surgery then? No. What is that honour? A word. What is in that word honour? What is that honour? Air. A trim reckoning!

Who hath it? He that died a-Wednesday. Doth he feel it? No. Doth he hear it? No. 'Tis insensible, then? Yea, to the dead. But will it not live with the living? No. Why. Detraction will not suffer it. Therefore I'll none of it. Honour is a mere scutcheon – and so ends my catechism. (*Henry IV Part I*, V.1.129–41)

S. L. Bethell's briefly incisive remarks on this will take us into its complexity.

This is one of the oldest sophistries, to confuse the notion signified with the signifying word. "What is that word honour? What is that honour? Air" *Flatus Vocis*, the extreme Nominalists said . . . It is the evacuation of all spiritual significance from life. (p.96)

Though we might disagree with Bethell's conclusion, nevertheless this observation directs us towards the significance of Falstaff's logic and rhetoric. The sceptical basis of Nominalism distrusted syllogistic logic as a means to truth. Universals were considered mental constructs only. Reality lay in things not words. Falstaff uses a sophistry for a provocative rhetorical end. Cause (honour) and effect (injuries and death) are conflated, juxtaposing the abstract and the concrete. By excluding intermediary explanatory propositions Falstaff confronts us with the brutal facts of war which forces us to face the question raised by all warfare. Does the invocation of a cause (patriotism, honour etc.) ever justify the reality of human suffering, or does the shock of the effect call into question the validity of the cause, forcing us to see it as an ideological simplification for something more complex and less ennobling: in this case power struggles arising from dynastic rivalries.

Of course, the speech can be taken in a more naturalistic way, in terms of Falstaff's character, as a witty rationalisation of his own self-preservation ('Give me life' *Henry IV Part I*, V.4.59). A longstanding formulaic view, considered above, is that Hotspur and Falstaff represent the excess and deficiency of honour while Hal realises the Aristotelian golden mean. There is a point here, but if Falstaff's speech is taken beyond that of character it obviously makes a critical point about the context of honour, name and fame – the anonymous carnage of those who are 'food for powder' (*Henry IV Part I*, IV.2.65–6). Even this has proved controversial. Is it a gross instance of Falstaff's exploitation and corruption or is it, as

Jorgensen (3) has shown, Shakespeare's use of Falstaff to represent a common military abuse of the time? There are so many aspects to Falstaff: he has been seen, variously, as a Renaissance sceptic (Chauduri); humanist 'fool' (Kaiser); holy fool (Battenhouse); Elizabethan soldier (Draper); carnival (Rhodes); morality vice and devil (Dover Wilson); Lord of Misrule (Barber); clown (Wiles); anthropological scapegoat (Stewart); narcissistic libido (Alexander); declassed feudal retainer (Jackson); bourgeois ego (Holderness 2). The list could be extended considerably, but underlying all of these is Falstaff as a comic performance. That is to say, most of the above categories are critical and intellectual abstractions mostly derived from the text, rather than performance. As Calderbank reminds us, Falstaff is a creation of and for the stage. He has a *relationship* to the Elizabethan world, to dramatic forebears, and to history, but his reality, his life, is the reality of comic stage performance. The role of Falstaff is multidimensional. Comedy establishes a mutual compact between actor and audience. Falstaff acts as much on behalf of the audience as on that of the plot. Downstage, playing to the audience Falstaff stands midway between the 1590s and the fifteenth century. The whole point about the encounter in the Boar's Head after the Gadshill fiasco is that everyone is made party to the comic set-up – Hal, Poins, Falstaff, and the audience. The Gadshill incident certainly has serious parodic undertones but from 'A plague on all cowards, I say' (*Henry IV Part I*, II.4.111ff) onwards, the scene builds upon the comic momentum of Falstaff's theatrical posture of self-righteousness undermined by incremental exaggeration. The progression is shaped by the design of protest, exposure and comic reversal – 'By the Lord, I knew ye as well as he that made ye' (*Henry IV Part I*, II.4.263) – not naturalism. Falstaff's 'cowardice' at Gadshill is a necessary circumstantial precondition to prime audience expectation, engineered by Hal, the 'interior' playwright as Calderbank calls him. Comic cowardice and cowardice normally considered are simply not the same thing, and should not be judged as such.

Superimposed on history Falstaff becomes the metadramatic figure of art itself free from the empirical constraints of chronicle, challenging the ideal ethos of chivalric honour. Falstaff's comedy is not just a matter of his verbal wit. Comedy creates a duality which checks simple moral judgement. As such the presentation of Falstaff is not unique in the plays. Shakespeare provides a dualistic perspective on almost every main character.

Over the dead Hotspur, Hal bids 'Adieu, and take thy praise with
thee to heaven!/Thy ignominy sleep with thee in the grave' (*Henry
IV Part I*, V.4.98–9). 'Praise' yet censure, 'ignominy' – the audience
has relished Hotspur's own particular comic exuberance throughout, as well as recognising his dangerous egotism. Hotspur's wife
provides a moving epitaph in *Henry IV Part II* (II.3.18–32), but we
have always been made aware of the political danger of such blind
rashness. Hotspur is, in turn, the embodiment of knighthood and its
abuser. Similarly, Douglas is jeered at by Hal (*Henry IV Part I*,
II.4.338–44), yet pardoned after Shrewsbury for his chivalric valour.
Hal is celebrated by Vernon's glowing evocation in a panegyric unrivalled in Shakespeare ('I saw young Harry with his beaver on',
Henry IV Part I, IV.1.104ff), yet he is commonly censured for his
calculation and lack of warmth. However, the claims of birth and
kingship have to be met, and however we react to the manner of
Falstaff's rejection, Hal as Henry V could hardly do otherwise in the
circumstances. Similarly with King Henry himself, either he allowed
Richard to seize his inheritance or he returned to England to claim
it, which of necessity entailed confrontation with the king and all
that followed. Either way Henry's feudal peers could not let Richard
get away with what was not a singular instance, but the culmination
of irreversible political abuse. What he did once he could do again.
Whatever we feel about the personal shortcomings of Henry we
recognise that he has to act politically as he does, or go under. From
one point of view he is a usurper, from another he is preserving the
country from anarchy. Though Jorgensen (4) has provided evidence
that not only was the Gaultree treachery hardly unique as a political
strategy, but that divine sanction was claimed for such acts,
nevertheless no commentators exonerate Prince John. Yet within the
play he is congratulated for his valour at Shrewsbury by Hal and
Henry (*Henry IV Part I*, V.4.16–23). 'Praise' and 'ignominy' again.

This duality occasionally structures whole scenes, if not both
plays when we consider the relationship of comedy and chronicle,
and 'travesty-by-parallel'. Consider Act III scene 1 of *Henry IV Part
I*. The rebels are assembled at Bangor to plan the carving up of the
country after the presumed success of their rebellion. A politically
self-indicting scene of great seriousness, yet from the outset a comic
circumstance – Hotspur has mislaid the map – is developed by
Hotspur's hilarious mockery of the pompous Glendower. Then
suddenly the mood is reversed as Lord Mortimer outlines the

division of the kingdom and Hotspur queries his portion (ll.66–114). To effect a transition Shakespeare uses Hotspur's humour to modify the tone (ll.115–58), again at Glendower's expense. Lord Mortimer redresses the balance by presenting a brief encomium on Glendower (ll.159–70), and Worcester follows this with a crushing epitome of Hotspur's faults (ll.177–83) – both examples of the dualistic points of view taken on all the main characters by themselves, or others, throughout the plays, but of course pre-eminently in the play-acting scene (*Henry IV Part I*, II.4) with Falstaff-as-king on Falstaff, and Hal-as-king on Falstaff. The rest of Act III scene 1, with the entry of the ladies, is like a scene from an early comedy with the contrasted pairs: the lovers, Lord Mortimer and Glendower's daughter, romantic, poetic and moving; the husband and wife, Hotspur and Lady Percy, ironic, gamesome and down-to-earth.

This ramified duality in character, scene and structure derives from compounded cultural factors. Christian civilisation fostered the notion of fallen man as a mixture of good and evil. Madeleine Doran has examined how the medieval debate influenced Renaissance drama in sustaining opposed ethical points of view in the same character. Neoclassical humanism re-emphasised this with its inheritance of deliberative rhetoric encouraging examination of the fors and againsts in any situation. This approach puts us in a better position to understand Falstaff, particularly in something like the stabbing of Hotspur.

The action is dualistic. In parodic functional terms it offers the counterpart to Hal's chivalric gesture over the dead Hotspur ('But let my favours hide thy mangled face', *Henry IV Part I*, V.4.95), and signalises Falstaff's succumbing to honour and reputation. As the comic performance in part surrenders to the imperatives of history so it is corrupted by it – to some extent. The character Falstaff is now drawn into the consequences of history by the burden of his acquired reputation and he enters the contingent world of time. Shakespeare stresses time as successive events, the matter of the chronicles, but Falstaff has lived a daily life of cocooned indulgence. Now the body is subject to time as Falstaff is caught up in the linear progression of history. In contrast a seasonal recurrent time of a continuing world outside the rise and fall of great ones is suggested by the Gloucestershire scenes – the sowing of the hade land, the bringing of beasts to market. The king dies, but nevertheless '. . . praise God for the merry year' (*Henry IV Part II*, V.3.18). Hal may wish to redeem time but the greater, all-encompassing truth, is that we owe God a death. The debt Falstaff recognises /'do not bid me remember mine end' (*Henry IV Part II*, II.4.232) is towards the living; the debt, obligation and relationship he feels for Hal, as well as for Poins and Bardolph. Like the fallen angels, Falstaff is never entirely without his own comedic gleam of light, however tarnished.

After the Gadshill robbery Hal and Poins, waiting for the return of their cohorts amuse themselves with Francis the drawer in the Boar's Head tavern. As indirect self-reproach Hal the 'truant' from chivalry attempts to make Francis a truant from his obligation and duty as apprentice, with the temptation of a thousand pounds, the seductive figure Mistress Quickly claims Falstaff says is owed to him by Hal, and the figure Falstaff acknowledges at the rejection, 'Master Shallow, I owe you a thousand pound' (*Henry IV Part II*, V.5.73). Roundly rebuked and rejected by Henry V, no longer Hal, Falstaff cannot say what he wants to say and so deflects it into the oblique utterance concerning the debt to Justice Shallow. His acknowledgement works on many levels, including a masterful insight into the psychology of shock. Until he succumbs to reputation, Falstaff has never recognised the validity of the claims of the public world. His order of value has always depended on the private and personal. The confrontation of the two men is a confrontation of these two worlds: Falstaff and Co, sweaty and unkempt, and the king in coronation robes nobly attended from Westminster Abbey.

In Henry V's words of rejection Franklin B. Newman finds that the king provides an example of 'rigorous charity' as laid down in the second part of the 'Sermon on Charity' from the *Homilies*. Of the two offices of charity the first is

to cheryshe good & harmelesse men, not to oppresse them wt false accusatiõs, but to encourage thẽ with rewardes to do wel & to cõtinue in wel doing.

The second Newman feels applies to Falstaff:

to rebuke, correct, and punyshe vyce, wythout regarde of persons, and is to be used agaynst theym onely, that be evil men and malefactors and evil doers. (p.154)

Henry thereby 'becomes palpably a king of charity: Shakespeare thus aligns him with sound governmental policy. Also Shakespeare aligns him with the highest Christian policy for a King, Prince, Father or Magistrate ...' (p.154). Newman only has half an argument, for Falstaff's reply at the rejection obliquely counters this with another kind of charity. What Falstaff wants to say has been said before in Eastcheap in the scene we have touched on already:

> *Host*   [Falstaff] said this other day you ought him a thousand pound.
> *Prince* Sirrah, do I owe you a thousand pound?
> *Hal*   A thousand pound, Hal? A million, thy love is worth a million, thou owest me thy love.
>
> *(Henry IV Part I*, III.3.132–36)

At the rejection Falstaff, recognising the king's righteous posture, wants to say 'Hal, you owe me your love', but he knows he cannot. In Eastcheap Falstaff had been using his pious puritan posture in echoing St Paul to evade answering the question by amusing Hal, yet at the same time giving voice to his real feelings, the satirical pre-empting any direct affective appeal.

The passage echoed is from St Paul's epistle to the Romans, chapter 13, immediately following one of the most well-known sources of political comment for the Middle Ages and the Renaissance in the whole of the Bible: 'Let every soule be subject unto the higher powers: for there is no power but of God: and the powers that be, are ordeined of God' (Geneva Bible). Thus begins the chapter seized on by royalists, monarchists and absolutists with its following complementary doctrine of non-resistance to 'the minister of God' (v.4). In fact when we turn to the homily on charity quoted by Franklin above, it is precisely this passage which is used to reinforce the two offices of charity. Through Falstaff Shakespeare turns the tables on this rigoristic charity prescription by appealing to experience itself. In terms of debt and obligation St Paul continues

> Give to all men therefore their duetie: tribute, to whom yee owe tribute: custome to whom custome; feare, to whom feare: honour, to whom ye owe honour. (v.7)

Here is found that alignment of debt and honour which we have seen is central to an understanding of *Henry IV Parts I & II*. Hal stands before Falstaff as Henry V, the English Caesar, one of the higher powers, sternly rebuking his old associate in this identifiable fashion. Though shocked, Falstaff's mind registers the situation and seizes on St Paul's larger intuition of charity. As the epistle proceeds St Paul turns from the contemporary historical world of Caesar, with its local political obligations, to the larger universal Christian ordinance of charity to which all men, Caesar, citizens and slaves, are bound.

Owe nothing to any man, but to love another: for he that loveth another, hath fulfilled the Lawe. (v.8)

This is the verse Falstaff had mimicked earlier '. . . thou owest me thy love', which is now deflected into 'Master Shallow, I owe you a thousand pound'.

Though his argument is bizarre in places, W. H. Auden's intuition of Falstaff as an embodiment of charity was at least taking the right direction, but he needed to register a few necessary caveats. Shakespeare's irony has Falstaff both burlesque and yet act as vehicle for this 'love'. The burlesque derives from the obvious inconsistency in Falstaff's overall behaviour when measured against St Paul. Falstaff's love is not the disinterested love of Christian charity, but it is closer to it than anything Hal says, which sounds inevitably Pharisaical. The very partiality of Falstaff's affections glow like Bardolph's nose in a world increasingly darkened by loveless relationships of power, possession and property, the exchange and mart of feudal honour. Fulfilment of either Christian charity or chivalric honour is fraught by egoism and hypocrisy, self-interest and necessity. But Falstaff's oblique avowal of love is the reverse of Prince John's blatant betrayal of honour, which is paralleled by Hal's betrayal of love.

'Sweet wag . . . sweet wag . . . mad wag . . . the most comparative rascalliest sweet young prince' (*Henry IV Part I*, I.2.16–79). In the first scene it is difficult to construe this as anything other than a manifestation of affection which betokens something deeper. Similarly, immediately before the rejection, it is hard to take Falstaff's excited anticipation at anything other than face value. It is true that Shakespeare shapes a crescendo for dramatic ends – it is the most long-awaited dramatic moment in the two plays – but we are not merely witnesses, the purely dramatic equally engages us as audience with Falstaff's emotions:

God save thy Grace, King Hal, my royal Hal! . . .
God save thee, my sweet boy! . . .
My King! My jove! I speak to thee, my heart!

I know thee not old man.
(Henry IV Part II, V.5.41–47)

To call the build-up to this cynical is cynical in itself. It would have
been cynical if Falstaff *had* 'bestowed the thousand pound' on 'new
liveries' (ll. 11–12). The drama of the confrontation is shaped by the
audience's emotional compact both with Falstaff and the new king:
emotion, psychology and situation are heightened by precise dramatic
antitheses – travel-stained clothing and coronation robes: im-
petuousness and formality: personal claims and impersonal duty:
private 'love' and public conduct: disorder, order: comedy and
innocence, seriousness and experience. Two laws collide, the in-
evitability of Falstaff's own nature and necessity of state. Relegating
Falstaff's parasitic qualities, drama has always bestowed the superior endowment of comic generosity, and however we regard Hal's
personal character, the leading imperatives of kingship must super-
vene, at least in the public actual world of both the chronicles and
the 1590s. But in the dramatic world of *Henry IV Parts I & II*
Shakespeare intimates a humanist revision of the actual by enlisting
the audience in a rejection of history for the sake of Falstaff.
Emotional impetus is stronger than public sanction. Prince John's
offstage valour never compensates for his onstage perfidy so who
could possibly agree with his closing remark endorsing the rejection,
'I like this fair proceeding of the King's' (l. 97)? Shakespeare knew
the answer to this. The epilogue plays with the idea of the audience
as creditor owed a successful play. On the contrary, by the end of
Henry IV Parts I & II Shakespeare knows that we are in Falstaff's
debt, and we owe him our love.

Texts

Hemingway, S. B. (ed.), *Henry IV, Part 1* (New Variorum Shakespeare, Philadelphia and London, 1936).

Shaaber, Matthias A. (ed.), *Henry IV, Part 2* (New Variorum Shakespeare, Philadelphia and London, 1940).

Humphreys, A. R. (ed.), *Henry IV, Part 1* (Arden Shakespeare, London, 1960).

Humphreys, A. R. (ed.), *Henry IV, Part 2* (Arden Shakespeare, London, 1966).

Davison, P. H. (ed.), *Henry IV, Part 1* (New Penguin Shakespeare, Harmondsworth, 1968).

Davison, P. H. (ed.), *Henry IV, Part 2* (New Penguin Shakespeare, Harmondsworth, 1977).

Mack, Maynard (ed.), *Henry IV, Part 1* (Signet Shakespeare, New York, 1965, 1987).

Holland, Norman L. (ed.), *Henry IV, Part 2* (Signet Shakespeare, New York, 1965).

Bevington, David (ed.), *Henry IV, Part 1* (Oxford Shakespeare, Oxford, 1987).

Melchiori, Giorgio (ed.), *Henry IV, Part 2* (Oxford Shakespeare, Oxford, 1989).

The New Variorum Shakespeare editions are monumental works of scholarship for reference only. All the remaining editions cater for students' needs with critical introductions, notes, sources and so on. Long established with footnotes that are easily used, the Arden edition has always been very popular. The Signet and Penguin editions have made their mark and are quite economical. The recent Oxford editions have excellent illustrations and are strong on stage history.

Bibliographies, Guides and Surveys

Bergeron, David M., and De Sousa, Geraldo U., *Shakespeare: A Study and Research Guide* (Lawrence, Kansas, 1987).

Berry, Edward, 'Twentieth-century Shakespeare criticism: the histories' in Stanley Wells (ed.), *The Cambridge Companion to Shakespeare Studies* (Cambridge, 1986).

Burden, Dennis H., 'Shakespeare's History Plays: 1952–1983', *Shakespeare Survey* 38, 1985, pp. 1–18.

Champion, Larry S., 'The English History Plays' in *The Essential Shakespeare. An Annotated Bibliography of Major Modern Studies* (Boston, 1986).

Dorius, R. J. (ed.), *Twentieth Century Interpretations of Henry IV Part One* (Englewood Cliffs, N.J., 1970).

Dutton, Richard, 'The Second Tetralogy' in Stanley Wells (ed.) *Shakespeare. A Bibliographical Guide* (New Edition, Oxford, 1990).

Hunter, G. K. (ed.), *Henry IV. Parts 1 and 2: A Casebook* (London, 1970).

Jenkins, Harold, 'Shakespeare's History Plays: 1900–1951', *Shakespeare Survey* 6, 1953, pp. 1–15.

Merrix, Robert P., 'Shakespeare's histories and The New Bardolators', *Studies in English Literature* 19, 1979, pp. 179–96.

Powell, Raymond, 'Henry IV' in *Shakespeare and the Critics Debate* (London, 1980).

Young, David P. (ed.), *Twentieth Century Interpretations of Henry IV Part Two* (Englewood Cliffs, N.J., 1968).

Wells, Robin Headlam, 'The Fortunes of Tillyard: Twentieth-Century Critical Debate in Shakespeare's History Plays', *English Studies*, 66, 1985, pp. 391–403.

References

Alexander, Franz, 'A Note on Falstaff', *Psychoanalytic Quarterly*, 1933, vol. 3, pp. 592–606.

Allen, J. W., *A History of Political Thought in the Sixteenth Century* (London, 1928).

Auden, W. H., 'The Prince's Dog' in *The Dyer's Hand* (London, 1948).

Babcock, Robert W., 'Mr Dover Wilson, the Critics and Falstaff', *The Shakespeare Association Bulletin* XIX, 1944, pp. 117–131.

Bakhtin, Mikhail, *Rabelais and His World* (Cam., Mass., 1968).

Barber, C. L., *Shakespeare's Festive Comedy* (Princeton, N.J., 1959).

Bate, Jonathan, *Shakespearean Constitutions, Politics, Theatre, Criticism 1730–1830* (Oxford, 1989).

Battenhouse, Roy, 'Falstaff as Parodist and Perhaps Holy Fool', *PMLA*, 90–1, 1975, pp. 32–52.

Bentley, G. E., *Shakespeare and Jonson. Their Reputations in the Seventeenth Century Compared*, 2 vols (Chicago, 1945).

Bethell, S. L., 'The Comic Element in Shakespeare's Histories', *Anglia*, 71, 1952–3, pp. 82–101.

Boas, F. S., *Shakespeare and His Predecessors* (London, 1896).

Boswell, James, *Life of Samuel Johnson*, 6 vols, ed. G. B. Hill and L. F. Powell (Oxford, 1934).

Bradley, A. C., *Oxford Lectures on Poetry* (Oxford, 1909).

Brandes, Georg, *William Shakespeare. A Critical Study*, 2 vols (London, 1898).

Bristol, Michael D., *Carnival and Theatre* (London, 1985).

Calderbank, James L., *Metadrama in Shakespeare's Henriad* (Berkeley, Calif., 1979).

Campbell, Lily B., *Shakespeare's Histories: Mirrors of Elizabethan Policy* (San Marino, California, 1947).

Capell, Edward, *Notes and Various Readings to Shakespeare* (1774). See Vickers (5).

Chauduri, Sukanta, *Infirm Glory: Shakespeare and the Renaissance Image of Man* (Oxford, 1981).

Clarke, Mary Cowden, *The Girlhood of Shakespeare's Heroines* (London, 1850–52).

Coleridge, S. T., *Coleridge on Shakespeare*, ed. R. A. Foakes (London, 1971).

Collier, Jeremy, *A Short View of the Immorality, and Profaness of the English Stage* (1698). See Vickers (2).

Courtenay, Thomas Peregrine, *Commentaries on the Historical Plays of Shakespeare*, 2 vols (London, 1840).

Cumberland, Richard, *The Observer* (1786). See Vickers (6).

Danby, John F., *Shakespeare's Doctrine of Nature* (London, 1949).

Davies, Thomas, *Dramatic Miscellanies* (1784). See Vickers (6).

Dennis, John, see Vickers (2).

Dering, Sir Edward. For the Dering Manuscript see under Halliwell-Phillips.

Dollimore, Jonathan and Alan Sinfield (eds), *Political Shakespeare* (Manchester, 1985).

Doran, Madeleine, *The Endeavours of Art* (Madison, Wisconsin, 1954).

Dowden, Edward, *Shakespeare His Mind and Art* (London, 1875).

Draper, John W., 'Sir John Falstaff', *Review of English Studies*, 8, 1932, pp. 414–24.

Dryden, John, 'An Essay on Dramatic Poesie' (1668). See Vickers (1).

Dryden, John, 'The Grounds of Criticism in Tragedy' in 'The Preface to Troilus and Cressida' (1679). See Vickers (1).

Dutton, Richard, 'The Second Tetralogy' in *Shakespeare: A Bibliographical Guide*, ed. Stanley Wells (Oxford, 1990).

Empson, William, *Essays on Shakespeare* (Cambridge, 1986).

Fermor, Una Ellis, 'Shakespeare's Political Plays' in *The Frontiers of Drama* (London, 1945).

Fineman, Daniel A., *Maurice Morgann, Shakespearian Criticism* (Oxford, 1972).

Frey, David L., *The First Tetralogy. Shakespeare's Scrutiny of the Tudor Myth* (Mouton, 1976).

Gentleman, Francis, Introduction & notes to Bell's edition of Shakespeare (1774). See Vickers (6).

Gervinus, G. G., *Shakespeare Commentaries* (new edition, revised London, 1875).

Gould, Gerald, 'A New Reading of *Henry IV*', *The English Review*, vol. 29, 1919, pp. 42–55.

Greenblatt, Stephen, 'Invisible Bullets' in *Shakespearean Negotiations* (Oxford, 1988).

Griffith, Elizabeth, *The Morality of Shakespeare's Drama illustrated* (1775). See Vickers (6).

Guthrie, William, *An Essay upon English Tragedy* (1747). See Vickers (3).

Halliwell-Phillips, James O., *Shakespeare's Play of Henry IV Printed from a Contemporary Manuscript* (London, 1945) [The Dering Manuscript].

Hart, Alfred, *Shakespeare and the Homilies* (Melbourne, 1934).

Hawkins, Sherman H., 'Henry IV: The Structural Problem Revisited', *Shakespeare Quarterly*, 33, 1982, pp. 278–301.

Hazlitt, William, *Characters of Shakespeare's Plays* (London, 1903).

Heath, Benjamin, *On Restoring Shakespeare's Text* (1765). See Vickers (4).

Holderness (1), Graham, 'Agincourt 1944: Readings in the Shakespeare Myth', *Literature and History*, 10 (1984), pp. 24–45.

Holderness (2), Graham, *Shakespeare's History* (Dublin, 1985).

Holderness (3), Graham, *Shakespeare: The Play of History* (London, 1988).

Hudson, H. N., *Shakespeare: His Life, Art and Characters* 2 vols (New York, 1848).

Jackson, T. A., 'Marx and Shakespeare', *Labour Monthly*, 1964, vol. 46, pp. 165–73.

Jenkins, Harold, 'The Structural Problem in Shakespeare's Henry IV' (1956) rep. in G. K. Hunter (ed.), *Henry IV Parts One and Two: A Casebook* (London, 1970), pp. 154–73.

Jefferson, D. W., '*Tristram Shandy* and the Tradition of Learned Wit', *Essays in Criticism*, vol. 1, No. 3, pp. 225–48.

Johnson, Dr Samuel, *The Plays of William Shakespeare* (1765). See Vickers (5).

Jorgensen (1), Paul A., 'Accidental Judgments, Casual Slaughters, and Purposes Mistook: Critical Reactions to Shakespeare's *Henry the Fifth*', *Shakespeare Association of America Bulletin*, vol. 22, 1947, pp. 51–61.

Jorgensen (2), Paul A., ' "Redeeming Time" in Henry IV' in *Redeeming Shakespeare's Words* (Berkeley, California, 1962).

Jorgensen (3), Paul A., *Shakespeare's Military World* (Berkeley and Los Angeles, 1956).

Jorgensen (4), Paul A., 'The "Dastardly Treachery" of Prince John of Lancaster', *PMLA*, 76–1, 1961.

Kaiser, Walter, *Praisers of Folly: Erasmus, Rabelais, Shakespeare* (London, 1964).

Kelly, H. A., *Divine Providence in the England of Shakespeare's Histories* (Cam., Mass., 1970).

Knights, L. C., 'Notes on Comedy', *Scrutiny* I, 1932–33, pp. 356–67.

Langbaum, Robert, 'Character versus Action in Shakespeare' in *The Poetry of Experience* (New York, 1957).

Lukács, Georg, 'Shakespeare and Historicism' from *The Historical Novel* (1962) in *Marxism and Art* (Brighton, 1979) ed. Maynard Soloman.

Lull, Ramon, *The Book of the Ordre of Chyvalry of Knyghthode* (London, 1926).

Lyttelton, Lord, *Dialogues of the Dead* (1760). See Vickers (4).

Mackenzie, Henry, *The Lounger* (1786). See Vickers (6).

Maginn, William, *Shakespearean Papers: Pictures Grave and Gay* (London, 1859).

Masefield, John, *William Shakespeare* (London, 1911).

Marriott (1), J. A. R., 'Shakespeare and Politics', *Cornhill Magazine*, New Series, vol. 63, 1927, pp. 678–90.

Marriott (2), J. A. R., *English History in Shakespeare* (London, 1918).

Montagu, Elizabeth, *An Essay on the Writings and Genius of Shakespeare* (1769). See Vickers (5).

Morgann, Maurice, *An Essay on the Dramatic Character of Falstaff* (1777). See Vickers (6). A full scholarly edition is that of Daniel A. Fineman (see above).

Morris, Corbyn, *An Essay Towards Fixing the True Standards of Wit* . . . (1744). See Vickers (3).

Munro, John, *The Shakespeare Allusion Book. A Collection of Allusions to Shakespeare from 1591 to 1700*, 2 vols (Oxford, 1932).

Murphy, Arthur, *London Chronicle: or Universal Evening Post* (1757). See Vickers (4).

Newman, Franklin B., 'The Rejection of Falstaff and the Religious Charity of the King', *Shakespeare Studies* II, 1966, pp. 162–173.

Odell, George C. D., *Shakespeare from Betterton to Irving*, 2 vols (New York, 1920).

Ornstein, Robert, *A Kingdom for a Stage* (Cam., Mass., 1972).

Poindexter, James Edward, *Criticism of Falstaff to 1860* (North Carolina, 1949) [unpublished Phd thesis].

Powell, Raymond, 'Henry IV' in *Shakespeare and the Critics' Debate. A Guide for Students* (London, 1980).

Prior, Moody E., *The Drama of Power: Studies in Shakespeare's History Plays* (Evanston, Ill., 1973).

Raleigh, Sir Walter, *Shakespeare* (London, 1907).

Reed, Robert Rentoul, *Crime and God's Judgment in Shakespeare* (Kentucky, 1984).

Reese, M. M., *The Cease of Majesty* (London, 1961).

Rhodes, Neil, *Elizabethan Grotesque* (London, 1980).

Ribner, Irving, *The English History Play in the Age of Shakespeare* (rev. ed. London, 1965).

Richardson, William, *Essays on Shakespeare's Dramatic Character of Sir John Falstaff* ... (1788). See Vickers (6).

Richmond, H. M., *Shakespeare's Political Plays* (New York, 1967).

Robertson, J. M., *Montaigne and Shakespeare* (London, 1897).

Rossiter, A. P., 'Ambivalence: The Dialectic of the Histories' in *Angel With Horns* (London, 1961).

Rowe, Nicholas, *Some Account of the Life etc. of Mr William Shakespeare* (prefixed to the 6 vol. edition of Shakespeare) 1709. See Vickers (2).

Rymer, Thomas, see Vickers (1 and 2).

Sabine, George H., *A History of Political Theory* (London, 1937).

Schlegel, A. W., *Lectures on Dramatic Art and Literature* (London, 1900).

Shaw, G. B., *Dramatic Opinions and Essays* (London, 1907).

Smirnov, A. A., *Shakespeare: A Marxist Interpretation* (New York, 1936).

Spencer, Hazleton, *Shakespeare Improved. The Restoration Versions in Quarto on the Stage* (New York, 1927, rep. 1963).

Spivack, Bernard, *Shakespeare and the Allegory of Evil* (New York, 1958).

Sprague, Arthur Colby, *Shakespeare's Histories. Plays for the Stage* (London, 1964).

Stack, Richard, 'An Examination of an Essay on the Dramatic Character of Sir John Falstaff ...' (1788). See Vickers (6).

Stewart, J. I. M., *Character and Motive in Shakespeare* (London, 1949).

Stoll, E. E., *Shakespeare Studies* (New York, 1927).

Stone, William B., 'Literature and Class Ideology: Henry IV, Part One', *College English*, vol. 33, 1972, pp. 891–900.

Stříbný, Zdenek, 'The Idea and Image of Time', *Shakespeare Jahrbuch* iii, 1975, pp. 15–66.

Swinburne, A. C., *A Study of Shakespeare* (London, 1879).

Tillyard, E. M. W., *The Elizabethan World Picture* (London, 1943).

Tillyard, E. M. W., *Shakespeare's History Plays* (London, 1944).

Traversi, D. A., 'Henry IV – Part I', *Scrutiny* 15, 1947–8, pp. 24–35.

Traversi, D. A., 'Henry IV – Part II', *Scrutiny* 15, 1947–8, pp. 117–27.

Traversi, D. A., *Shakespeare: From 'Richard II' to 'Henry V'* (Stanford, California, 1951).

Tucker Brooke, E. F., *The Tudor Drama* (London, 1912).

Ulrici, Hermann, *Shakespeare's Dramatic Art* (London, 1876).

Vickers (ed.) 1, Brian, *Shakespeare: The Critical Heritage* vol. 1, 1626–1692 (London, 1974).

Vickers (ed.) 2, Brian, *Shakespeare: The Critical Heritage* vol. 2, 1693–1733 (London, 1974).

Vickers (ed.) 3, Brian, *Shakespeare: The Critical Heritage* vol. 3, 1733–1752 (London, 1975).

Vickers (ed.) 4, Brian, *Shakespeare: The Critical Heritage* vol. 4, 1753–1765 (London, 1976).

Vickers (ed.) 5, Brian, *Shakespeare: The Critical Heritage* vol. 5, 1765–1774 (London, 1979).

Vickers (ed.) 6, Brian, *Shakespeare: The Critical Heritage* vol. 6, 1774–1801 (London, 1981).

Walwyn, B., *An Essay on Comedy* (1782). See Vickers (6).

Warburton, William, Additional notes to Lewis Theobald's edition of Shakespeare (1733). See Vickers (2).

Wells, Robin Headlam, 'The Fortunes of Tillyard: Twentieth-Century Critical Debate on Shakespeare's History Plays', *English Studies* 66 (1985), pp. 391–403.

Wendell, Barrett, *William Shakespeare* (New York, 1894).

Wiles, David, *Shakespeare's Clown. Actor and Text in the Elizabethan Playhouse* (Cambridge, 1987).

Wilson, John Dover, *The Fortunes of Falstaff* (London, 1943).

Yeats, W. B., 'At Stratford-Upon-Avon' in *Essays and Introductions* (London, 1961).

Index